War under Sea

War Under Sea

Capt. (Retd.) Prem Singh

Prashant Publishing House
DELHI - 110094 (INDIA)

PRASHANT PUBLISHING HOUSE
C-34, 28 Foota Road, Gali No. 3
West Karawal Nagar, Delhi-110094
Phone : 9810396373, 22963970

War Under Sea

First Published : 2010

ISBN : 978-93-80565-08-8

PRINTED IN INDIA

Published by Mr. R. K. Jha M/s. Prashant Publishing House, Delhi and Printed at H.S. Offset Press, Delhi.

Preface

War under Sea is a strategic board wargame depicting the naval war in the Atlantic during World War II, It is also the basis for the design of the subsequent Avalon Hill game, Victory in the Pacific.

The first dateable recorded sea battle occurred about 1210 BC: Suppiluliuma II, king of the Hittites, defeated a fleet from Cyprus, and burned their ships at sea. Assyrian reliefs from the 700s BC show Phoenician fighting ships, with two levels of oars, fighting men on a sort of bridge or deck above the oarsmen, and some sort of ram protruding from the bow. No written mention of strategy or tactics seems to have survived. The Greeks of Homer just used their ships as transport for land armies, but in 664 BC there is a mention of a battle at sea between Corinth and its colony city Corcyra. The Persian Wars were the first to feature large-scale naval operations, not just sophisticated fleet engagements with dozens of triremes on each side, but combined land-sea operations. It seems unlikely that all this was the product of a single mind or even of a generation; most likely the period of evolution and experimentation was simply not recorded by history.

A naval force has command of the sea when it is so strong that its rivals cannot attack it directly. Also called sea control, this dominance may apply to its surrounding waters (i.e., the littoral) or may extend far into the oceans, meaning the country has a blue-water navy. It is the naval equivalent of air superiority. With command of the sea, a country (or alliance) can ensure that its own military and merchant ships can move around at will, while its rivals are forced either to stay in port or to try to evade it.

The book is meant for detailing and analysing the War under Sea, students deply known its matters.

—Editor

Contents

Preface

1. Introduction 1
2. Great War at Sea Series 12
3. Submarine Warfare 43
4. Nuclear Weapon 102
5. Fire and Capital Ship 161
6. Ballistic and Anti-ship Missile 182
7. Indian Navy 198
8. Types of Navy in Difference Countries 219
9. Naval Mine 259
10. Sonar 307

Bibliography 327

Index 328

1

Introduction

War under Sea is a strategic board wargame depicting the naval war in the Atlantic during World War II, It is also the basis for the design of the subsequent Avalon Hill game, Victory in the Pacific.

GAME SUMMARY

Units represented in the game are individual ships of heavy cruiser size or larger, with provisions also given for convoys, submarines (specifically 'U-Boats'), and air power. Each turn represents a period of roughly six months. The board represents the Atlantic Ocean and the Mediterranean Sea, which are divided up into six zones. Control of as many of these zones as possible, for as many turns as possible, is the goal of the game. One player assumes the role of the Allied player, and controls the British, Soviet, and American navies. His or her opponent is the Axis player, and controls the German and Italian navies. In addition to the units representing individual ships, both players have one unit each that represents land-based airplane squadrons, and the Axis player has units that represent squadrons of U-boats.

Ships are represented by a single counter which typically gives three factors: gunnery, armour, and speed. While these are the essential statistics for surface vessels, this system keeps them all highly abstracted, as each is just a simple number, falling within a range of 0 to 9. Aircraft carriers have a fourth factor, representing the naval air-power on board. The land-based air units each represent three air attacks (against three different targets).

Each turn begins with both players' ships in ports. The Allied player's ports include England, the United States, Leningrad, "Russia" (actually Murmansk, on the Arctic Ocean), and Malta, in the Mediterranean. The Axis player's ports include Germany, France (after Turn Two, when it is assumed that Germany conquers France by land, just as it did in the real war), and Italy. Each turn, each player (the Allied player first, and then the Axis player) moves all, some, or none of his ships into sea areas that are adjacent to the port in which those ships started the turn. Ships can also attempt to move one additional sea area if the first area was not controlled by the enemy on the previous turn to accomplish that, the ship must roll a die and get a result less than that ship's speed factor. Ships that have a speed factor of seven or eight are thus automatically able to move two spaces, and are therefore very valuable. The proviso that the first area may not have been controlled by the enemy allows either player (usually the Allied player) to make certain that areas of the sea are unreachable to the enemy fleet due to intervening controlled areas. Ships that remain in port instead of moving are able to repair damage that they may have sustained in previous turns. When the Allied player is finished, the Axis player moves his ships. U-boats are able to move to any sea area and are therefore the only ships that cannot be blockaded by enemy control.

If only one player's ships occupy a sea area after movement is finished, that player controls the sea area for the turn, and he or she scores points for it (the number of points varies, depending on which sea area is controlled by which player). If there are ships from both sides in the same sea area, the two fleets must fight at least one round of combat.

Combat is resolved with each ship picking a target and rolling one die per gunnery factor, and each 'hit' (generally, a roll of six) is re-rolled to produce the amount of damage generated, which is applied to the target's armour factor. If the amount of damage exceeds the armour factor, the ship is sunk. Air attacks are resolved by rolling one die for each attack at a number of targets equal to the air factor. (Note that this system is somewhat similar to the combat system in Dungeons and Dragons, which also consists of target selection, a die roll 'to hit,' and, if a hit is scored, a second die roll to determine a number representing a level of damage. On a roll of five, the ship is disabled, which means that it is forced to return to port.

This method generates a lot of dice rolls, and gave the game the nicknames 'Dice at Sea' and 'Yahtzee at Sea', with critics arguing that it depended too much upon luck, and supporters countering that the high number of die rolls actually allows the luck to even out.

Minor rules include provisions for U-boat combat, the 'neutral port' of South America (which is where disabled ships in the South Atlantic sea area must go, and which they have to leave the following turn, lest the owning player lose points), convoys (which score additional points for the Allied player if they make it to England or Russia), and the possible internment of the Italian fleet if the Allies control the Mediterranean Sea for much of the game.

VARIATIONS

Numerous variations (or 'variants,' to use the word preferred by Avalon Hill) were published for *War at Sea* in the years since it was released. Many of them appeared in the General, Avalon Hill's house magazine. Among these variations are rules for the French Navy (which is interned early in the war), the Greek Navy, a third Russian port on the Black Sea, Allied mini-submarines (such as the 'X-craft' submarines that were used to attack the German battleship Tirpitz late in the war), and additional ships that were not represented in the original game. These variations add simulation detail to the game (meaning that they made it more like the real war at sea), but at the expense of making it slightly harder to playHeavy cruiser

The heavy cruiser was a type of cruiser, a naval warship designed for long range, high speed and an armament of naval guns roughly 203mm calibre (8 inches). The heavy cruiser can be seen as a lineage of ship design from 1915 until 1945, although the term 'heavy cruiser' only came into formal use in 1930. The heavy cruiser's immediate precursors were the light cruiser designs of the 1900s and 1910s, rather than the armoured cruisers of before 1905.

Evolution & Definition

At the end of the 19th century, cruisers were classified as First, Second or Third Class depending on their capabilities. First class Cruisers were typically armoured cruisers, hard to distinguish from a small pre-dreadnought battleship. The lighter, cheaper and faster Second and Third Class cruisers tended to have a protective armour deck, rather than armoured hulls, and hence were known as protected cruisers. In the first decade of the 20th century, the First Class Armoured Cruiser metamorphosed into the battlecruiser, and increased markedly in size and cost. At the same time, the Third Class Cruiser started to carry thin steel armour on the outside of its hull and became known as the light cruiser. The wide gap between the massive battlecruiser of perhaps 20,000 tons and 305 mm (12-inch) guns and the small light cruiser of up to 5,000 tons and 100 mm (4-in) or 155 mm (6-inch) guns naturally left scope for an intermediate type.

The first such design was the British 'Atlantic cruiser' proposal of 1912, which proposed a long-range cruiser of about 8,000 tons displacement with 190 mm (7.5-inch) guns. This was a response to a rumour that Germany was building cruisers to attack merchant shipping in the Atlantic with 170mm guns. The German raiders proved to be fictional and the 'Atlantic cruisers' were never built. However, in 1915 the requirement for long-range trade-protection cruisers resurfaced and resulted in the Hawkins class, which carried a 190 mm (7.5-inch) battery and had a displacement just under 10,000 tons.

The old armoured cruiser was not a close ancestor of these heavy cruiser models, even though the name sometimes suggests this. By 1905 the armoured cruiser had grown in size and power to be very close to the pre-dreadnought battleships of the day, with a displacement of around 15,000 tons: considerably larger than the 10,000 tons of the heavy cruiser. This trend resulted in the battlecruiser, which was initially conceived as an armoured cruiser on the same scale as the dreadnought battleship. By 1915, both battleships and battlecruisers had grown markedly; HMS *Hood*, for instance, designed at around that time, displaced 45,000 tons. The great gap between heavy cruisers and the capital ships of the same generation meant that, unlike the armoured cruiser, the heavy cruiser could not be expected to serve as a junior battleship.

There were also important technical differences between the heavy cruiser and the armoured cruiser which reflected the generational gap between them. Heavy cruisers, like all contemporary ships, were powered by steam turbine engines and were capable of far faster speeds than armoured cruisers had ever been. While the main armament of a heavy cruiser was smaller than the typical 233 mm (9.2-inch) guns of an armoured cruiser, the greater number of guns on the heavy cruiser and the introduction of fire control in the 1920s and 30s meant that the heavy cruiser was far more powerful.

Washington Treaty

The Washington Naval Treaty of 1921 introduced very strict limits on the construction of battleships and battlecruisers, defined as warships of more than 10,000 tons standard displacement or with armament of a calibre greater than eight inches (203 mm). Under this limit, far fewer restrictions applied. The 10,000 tons and 155 mm (6-inch) level was set with reference to the British *Hawkins* class, but both Japan and the USA were also considering designs on a similar specification. The Japanese model became the *Furutaka* class.

The emergence of these new, powerful cruiser classes sparked off something of a cruiser arms-race. The Japanese navy had a doctrine of building more powerful ships in every class than its likely opponents, which led to the development of several very impressive heavy cruiser classes. British and American building was more influenced by the desire to be able to match the Japanese ships while keeping enough cruisers for their other global responsibilities. With battleships heavily regulated by the Washington Treaty, and aircraft carriers not yet mature, the cruiser question became the focus of naval affairs. The British, with a strained economy and global commitments, favoured unlimited cruiser tonnage but strict limits on the individual ships. The Americans favoured the opposite: strictly limited numbers of powerful cruisers. Disagreements between the British and Americans wrecked the 1927 conference on naval affairs.

Even during the 1920s, the 10,000 ton limit was not strictly observed. British, French and American designers generally worked to the limit with precision. The Japanese *Myoko* class, however, grew during its construction as the naval general staff prevailed on the designers to increase the weapons load. As well as a breach of the Treaty, this was a poor decision from the design point of view and the ships had to be reconstructed in the 1930s to reduce weight. The German *Deutschland* class, which were technically armoured coast defence ships under the terms of the Treaty of Versailles, was in effect a heavy cruiser being upgunned to 11-inch batteries at the cost of slower speed; their displacement was declared at 10,000 tons but was in practice considerably bigger.

London Treaty

In 1930 the Washington Naval Treaty was extended by the London Naval Treaty, which finally settled the arguments on cruisers which had raged in the 1920s. The treaty defined limits on both *heavy cruisers*-those with guns larger than 155 mm (6.1 inches)-and *light cruisers*-those with smaller-calibre guns. The limit of 10,000 tons displacement still applied to both. This was the point at which the split between 'heavy' and 'light' cruisers finally became official and widespread.

The Treaty satisfied Britain and America. However, it deeply offended Japan, as this severely limited the numbers of heavy cruisers that the Imperial Japanese Navy could have, as they considered heavy cruisers as key warships in a line of battle with their 8-inch guns and heavy torpedo armament. The IJN placed less priority on purpose-built light cruisers, most of their existing types dating back to the 1920s (the five WWII-era light cruisers that the IJN commissioned were less well-armed than light cruisers of the US and Royal Navies), which were largely relegated to leading destroyer squadrons. The solution the Japanese adopted was to build the Mogami class, which was declared as a 10,000 ton light cruiser with fifteen 6.1-inch guns. In practice, they displaced over 12,000 tons, and it was always intended to replace her turrets to give a final armament of ten 203 mm guns, making something of a nonsense of the light and heavy cruiser classifications.

The German navy also paid lip-service to the treaty limitations, with the *Admiral Hipper* class weighing in at 14,000 tons.

In the mid 1930s, Britain, France and Italy ceased building heavy cruisers. It was felt that in a likely cruiser engagement, a larger number of 155 mm (6-inch) guns would be preferable to a smaller number of 203 mm (8-inch). The heavier shell of the 203 mm weapon was of little advantage, as most ships that could withstand a 6-inch hit were also well-protected against eight-inch shells. This led to the construction of cruisers up to the 10,000-tons limit, with twelve to fifteen 155 mm guns. While these ships fell into the 'light cruiser' classification by virtue of the calibre of their main armament, they were designed to fight a heavy cruiser on equal terms, again making something of a nonsense of the classifications.

The 1936 London Naval Treaty, principally negotiated between Britain and the United States but never ratified, abolished the heavy cruiser entirely by restricting new construction to 8,000 tons and 155 mm (6.1-inch) guns. This suited Britain's needs very well, but was largely a dead letter. The U.S. continued to build heavy cruisers, culminating in the *New Orleans* class and USS *Wichita*.

Second World War

Heavy cruisers were still being built, and they could be balanced designs when nations decided to skirt the restrictions imposed by the London Naval Treaty. The Germans built their *Hipper* class heavy cruisers of 14,000 tons, although the Anglo-German Naval Agreement was supposed to limit their shipbuilding.

The U.S. built the *Baltimore* class of heavy cruisers during the war. While earlier heavy cruisers were noted for their powerful torpedo armament (especially Japanese heavy cruisers), later ships built by the USN concentrated mainly on anti-aircraft armament as their main role was escorting aircraft carriers instead of engaging in surface actions. Interestingly, most Japanese heavy cruisers were sunk by aircraft or submarines, instead of surface engagements. The U.S. built the last heavy cruisers, which were finished shortly after the war. The *Baltimore* class consisted of seventeen ships, including six of the slightly different *Oregon City* class. The *Des Moines* class were the last heavy cruisers built, though based on the Baltimores, they were considerably heavier due to their new rapid-firing 203 mm (8-inch) guns. Additionally, two aircraft carriers were built on a *Baltimore*-derived hull, the *Saipan* class.

The largest heavy cruisers were the *Alaska* class of "large cruiser". Though they resembled contemporary battlecruisers or battleships in general appearance, as well as having main armament and displacement equal or greater than that of capital ships of the First World War, they were actually upscaled heavy cruisers. The *Alaskas,* for instance, lacked the armoured belt and torpedo defence system of true capital ships. They also had proportionately less weight in armour at 16% of displacement, similar to heavy cruisers, in contrast to the British battlecruiser *Hood* of 30%, and the German *Scharnhorst* and US *North Carolina* battleships of 40%. The layout of the *Alaskas* machinery and the possession of a single rudder was also based on that of cruisers rather than that of capital ships.

USS *Columbus* in 1965. Originally a Baltimore class cruiser, she was rebuilt into an Albany class guided missile cruiser. Heavy cruisers fell out of use after the Second World War. Some existing US heavy cruisers lasted until the 1970s, sometimes after conversion to guided missile cruisers (US hull symbol CG). The last heavy cruiser in existence (as of 2006) is the USS *Salem,* now a museum ship.

U-BOAT

U-boat is the anglicized version of the German word U-Boot (help·info), itself an abbreviation of Unterseeboot (undersea boat), and refers to military submarines operated by Germany, particularly in World War I and World War II. Although in theory, U-boats could have been useful fleet weapons against enemy naval warships, in practice they were most effectively used in an economic-warfare role (Commerce raiding), enforcing a naval blockade against enemy shipping. The primary targets of the U-boat campaigns in both wars were the merchant convoys bringing supplies from the British Empire and the United States to the islands of Great Britain. Austrian submarines of World War I were also known as U-boats.

The distinction between *U-boat* and *submarine* is common in English-language usage (where *U-boat* refers exclusively to the German vessels of the World Wars) but is unknown in German, in which the term *U-Boot* refers to any submarine.

Pre-War

The first submarine built in Germany was the *Brandtaucher*, designed in 1850 by the inventor and engineer Wilhelm Bauer and built by Schweffel & Howaldt in Kiel for the German Navy.

This was followed in 1890 by W1 and W2, built to a Nordenfelt design. In 1904, Krupp's dockyard in Kiel completed a submarine which was sold to Russia. The first works were carried out by the Spanish engineer Raymondo Lorenzo d'Equevilley Montjustin (submarine 'Narval'). The first unit for the German Navy was built in 1905. This was the "Karp" class which had a double hull, was powered by a Körting kerosene engine and armed with a single torpedo tube. It was designated *U-1*, with the 50% larger *U-2* design having two tubes. A diesel engine was not installed in a German Navy boat until the U-19 class of 1912–13. At the start of World War I, Germany had 48 submarines of 13 classes in service or under construction.

World War I

At the start of World War I, Germany had twenty-nine U-boats in service; in the first ten weeks, five British cruisers had been lost to them. In September, *U-9* sank the obsolete British warships *Aboukir*, *Cressy* and *Hogue* (the "Live Bait Squadron") in a single hour.

For the first few months of the war, U-boat anti-commerce actions observed the "prize rules" of the time which governed the treatment of enemy civilian ships and their occupants. On 20 October 1914, *U-17* sank the first merchant ship, the SS *Glitra*, off Norway. Surface commerce raiders were proving to be ineffective, and on 4 February 1915, the *Kaiser* assented to the declaration of a war zone in the waters around the British Isles. This was cited as a retaliation for British minefields and shipping blockades.

Under the instructions given to U-boat captains, they could sink merchant ships, even potentially neutral ones, without warning. A statement by the U.S. Government, holding Germany "strictly accountable" for any loss of American lives, made no material difference. On 7 May 1915, *U-20* sank the liner RMS *Lusitania* with a single torpedo hit. The sinking claimed 1,198 lives, 128 of them American civilians, including noted theatrical producer Charles Frohman and Alfred Vanderbilt, a member of the prestigious Vanderbilt family. The sinking deeply shocked the Allies and their sympathizers because an unarmed civilian merchant vessel was attacked. According to the ship's manifest, *Lusitania* was carrying military cargo. After further investigations, it has been confirmed that the Lusitania was in fact carrying bullets and ammunition for the allies to use against the Germans. However, this was not known at the time and the Lusitania was mistaken for a troopship. It was not until the sinking of the ferry "Sussex" that there was a widespread reaction in the USA.

The initial U.S. response was to threaten to sever diplomatic relations, which persuaded the Germans to re-impose restrictions on U-boat activity. The U.S. reiterated its objections to German submarine warfare whenever U.S. civilians died as a result of German attacks, which prompted the Germans to fully re-apply prize rules. This, however, removed the effectiveness of the U-boat fleet, and the Germans consequently sought a decisive surface action, a strategy which culminated in the Battle of Jutland.

Although the Germans claimed victory at Jutland, the British Grand Fleet remained in control at sea. It was necessary to return to effective anti-commerce warfare by U-boats. Vice-Admiral Reinhard Scheer, Commander in Chief of the High Seas Fleet, pressed for all-out U-boat war, convinced that a high rate of shipping losses would force Britain to seek an early peace before the United States could react effectively.

U-BOAT SINKING A TROOP TRANSPORT SHIP

The renewed German campaign was effective, sinking 1.4 million tons of shipping between October 1916 and January 1917. Despite this, the political situation demanded even greater pressure, and on 31 January 1917, Germany announced that its U-boats would engage in unrestricted submarine warfare beginning 1 February. On 17 March, German submarines sank three American merchant vessels, and the U.S. declared war on Germany in April 1917.

In the end, the German strategy failed to destroy sufficient Allied shipping, largely due to the introduction of escorted convoys, before U.S. manpower and materiel could be brought to bear in France. However, the main reason for the ending of the war was the effectiveness of the British blockade of Germany which brought about an economic collapse. An armistice became effective on 11 November 1918 and all surviving German submarines were surrendered. Of the 360 submarines that had been built, 178 were lost but more than 11 million tons of shipping had been sunk.

2

Great War at Sea Series

The *Great War at Sea* series of board wargames released by Avalanche Press features operational and tactical-level naval combat in the period of the early battleships and dreadnoughts (various titles cover from 1898-1930). Each game in the series comes with a common rule book and tactical map, as well as game-specific operational map, counters and scenarios.

There have been nine games in the series to date, and it was the basis for Avalanche's spin off series the *Second World War at Sea*, as well as a proposed new series dealing with ironclads. It has proven very popular, with the third game being Avalanche's sixth best selling title. Also, two of the titles have received Origins Awards.

Overview

The focus of *Great War at Sea* series games features two levels of play: the "operational" game, where fleets move and conduct missions on a map of the area where the game takes place (this map uses "staggered squares"—technically a hex grid—presumably to save space as the squares are the exact same size as the fleet counters, and only a few counters are on the board at a time); and the "tactical" game, where the individual ships maneuver and fire on a generic open sea tactical map.

Turns in the strategic segment are about 3 hours, and fleets are given missions when they set out. With many missions, the entire route and actions must be pre-plotted at the beginning, with some more flexible assignments (usually raiding or searching) only requiring two turns of advance planning. Each force is represented on the map with a single counter, so the composition is not known to the enemy. Raiding forces are not placed on the map until they do something (like attack merchant shipping), or is found by searching enemy forces. So, much of the game is spent with forces going about pre-determined missions while reaction forces attempt to find them and force them to battle, or to abort their mission.

Once two forces *do* find each other, combat is resolved by means of a light tactical system. Each ship bigger than a destroyer has its own counter, while destroyers and smaller vessels have counters that can represent one to three ships.

There is a certain amount of record-keeping in the system, with hits from combat being recorded against gunnery, hull or speed factors. Fuel is also tracked, with provisions for refueling in port as well as at sea. For combat, ships are primarily rated as having primary, secondary and tertiary gunnery factors, which have different ranges and ability to penetrate armour to do damage.

Boxed Games

Mediterranean: *Mediterranean* was the initial release in the series, and has been released in a second edition.

Northern Waters/Jutland: Originally released as *Great War at Sea: Northern Waters*, *Jutland* was released in December 2006 as a second revised edition of the original title.

U.S. Navy Plan Orange: The first of what would become a popular 'sub series' *Plan Orange* received the 1998 Origins Award for *Best Historical Board Game*. Studying the actual plans of the United States Navy and Imperial Japanese Navy, *Plan Orange* attempts to recreate what a war in the Pacific would have been like in 1930 if there had been no Washington Naval Treaty.

Set later than any other game in the series, it includes extra rules for dealing with air-to-air combat, and aircraft carriers. The operational map covers from Formosa (Taiwan) to Kyûshû and the northern Philippines.

The counter mix provides many of the forces that would historically have been available in 1930, as well as some of the battleships and battlecruisers that had been canceled due to the

Washington treaty, while those that had been converted to carriers because of the treaty still appear as such (except for the battleship *Kaga*, which appears as such, and the *Amagi* which was canceled after being wrecked in an earthquake, appears as a carrier).

Plan Orange is out of print and was planned to be released in a new version sometime in 2007 or 2008, but has since been postponed indefinitely.

1904-1905: The Russo-Japanese War: Covering the naval portions of the Russo-Japanese War, this volume received the 1999 Origins Award for *Best Historical Board Game.*

U.S. Navy Plan Black: *U.S. Navy Plan Black* was based on the plans developed for a conflict against Germany should she emerge victorious in WWI. It includes many ships canceled by the Versailles Treaty, and an operational map covering part of the Caribbean. As *Plan Gold* features a larger map covering the same area, *Plan Black* is out of print, and will not be reprinted, short of a major revision.

1898: The Spanish-American War: Detailing the naval actions of the Spanish-American War.

U.S. Navy Plan Red: Based on hypothetical War Plan Red for fighting the Royal Navy, and possible actions in Canada.

Cruiser Warfare: *Cruiser Warfare* is about merchant raiding in the early parts of WWI as practiced by long-range cruisers. Instead of a normal operational map, it features a world map, with different areas to move between.

U.S. Navy Plan Gold: Based on hypothetical plans for fighting the French Navy, *Plan Gold* features an operational map of the Caribbean. It was produced under Avalanche's *Classic Wargames* (preorder) program and was released in mid 2006.

Cone of Fire: *Cone of Fire* contains both *Great War at Sea* and *Second World War at Sea* pieces for South American nations. It was produced under the *Classic Wargames* program and was released in March 2008.

Pacific Crossroads: *Pacific Crossroads* is the new introductory game for *Great War at Sea* and covers a conflict between the United States and Japan during the early part of the 20th century. It uses a small box size and comes with a new edition of the series rules and shares a sheet of counters with *Coral Sea*.

Future Games

Three future *Great War at Sea* boxed games have been mentioned in the *Gold Club Insider* for inclusion in a future Classic Wargames round. The April 2008 Gold Club Insider also mentions an introductory Great War at Sea game to be announced sometime in 2008.

Downloadable Games

U.S. Navy Plan Crimson: *U.S. Navy Plan Crimson* was announced on October 22, 2008 as the first free downloadable game for Gold Club members. *Plan Crimson* covers a fictional conflict between the United States and Canada in the 1920s and features many "lake battleships". The game is only available to Gold Club members as a free download

Supplements

Great White Fleet: *Great White Fleet* was an early supplement to the series, with 20 new operational scenarios generally set from 1898 to 1908. They all require multiple products to play (usually the operational map from either *1898, 1905, Plan Orange* or *Plan Black,* as well as counters from one or more of those and *Northern Waters*). It has a more detailed battle system for pre-dreadnoughts (emphasizing command and control issues), as well as new (unmounted) counters on the back cover, and an operational map covering the southern Philippines (meant to connect with the *Plan Orange* map). As *Plan Orange, Plan Black, 1898* and *1904* are all out of print, Avalanche has let the book go out of print with no plans of making it available again.

Dreadnoughts: *Dreadnoughts* is another supplement for the entire line of *Great War at Sea* games, with counters for new ships, scenarios, and advanced rules for tactical combat. Dreadnoughts focuses on the South American dreadnoughts, such as Brazil's Minas Gerais class battleships, the Brazilian battleship Rio de Janeiro, Argentina's Rivadavia class battleship, and Chile's battleships. Several Austrian warships are also included, such as an aircraft carrier, the *Projekt V* class fast battleships, the *Projekt*

VI class light battlecruisers, some more cruisers, and some other battlecruisers. Spain's second and third generation dreadnoughts are also included, as are some Russian cruisers and Turkish battleships.

Zeppelins: *Zeppelins* is a supplement released in July 2007 with new 2/3" by 1 1/3" counters for various airships of different countries. It includes articles about airships, new rules for the use of these new airships and new or modified scenarios from previous games using the counters.

Sea of Troubles: *Sea of Troubles* is a new version of the old *Plan Red* game, but is set in the Caribbean Sea and uses the *Plan Gold* map. It was announced on November 19, 2007 and is scheduled to be released in December 2007. It contains the same pieces as the original game, including British G3 battlecruisers, N3 battleships, and the American 1919 class battleship.

Future Supplements

Avalanche Press has stated that it would like more *Great War at Sea* supplements to be available.

NAVAL WARFARE

Naval warfare is combat in and on seas, oceans, or any other major bodies of water such as large lakes and wide rivers.

History

Mankind has fought battles on the sea for more than 3,000 years. Land warfare would seem, initially, to be irrelevant and entirely removed from warfare on the open ocean, though this is not necessarily true. Land navigation, until the advent of extensive railroads was extremely dependent upon river systems and canals. The latter were crucial in the development of the modern world in the United Kingdom, the Low Countries and northern Germany, for they enabled the bulk movement of goods and raw materials without which the Industrial Revolution would not have occurred. Prior to 1750, things moved by barge or sea, or not much at all. Thus armies, with their exorbitant needs for food, ammunition and fodder, were tied to the river valleys throughout the ages. The oceanic influences throughout pre-recorded history (Homeric

Legends, e.g. Troy), and classical works like the *Odyssey* underscore the past influences. The Persian Empire — united and strong — couldn't prevail against the might of the Athenian fleet combined with that of lesser city states in several attempts to conquer the Greek city states. Phoenicia's and Egypt's power, Carthage's and even Rome's depended in no mean way upon control of the seas. So too did the Venetian Republic dominate Italy's city states, thwart the Ottoman Empire, and dominate commerce on the Silk Road and the Mediterranean in general for centuries. For three centuries, the Northmen commonly called the Vikings raided and pillaged and went where they willed, far into central Russia and the Ukraine, and even to far off Constantinople (both via the Black Sea tributaries and through the Strait of Gibraltar).

The many sea battles through history also provide a reliable source of shipwrecks for underwater archaeology. A major example, albeit not very commonly known, is the exploration of the wrecks of various battleships in the Pacific Ocean, namely Japanese warships that sank during the Battle of Midway.

Oars People of the Mediterranean Sea

The first dateable recorded sea battle occurred about 1210 BC: Suppiluliuma II, king of the Hittites, defeated a fleet from Cyprus, and burned their ships at sea. Assyrian reliefs from the 700s BC show Phoenician fighting ships, with two levels of oars, fighting men on a sort of bridge or deck above the oarsmen, and some sort of ram protruding from the bow. No written mention of strategy or tactics seems to have survived.

The Greeks of Homer just used their ships as transport for land armies, but in 664 BC there is a mention of a battle at sea between Corinth and its colony city Corcyra. The Persian Wars were the first to feature large-scale naval operations, not just sophisticated fleet engagements with dozens of triremes on each side, but combined land-sea operations. It seems unlikely that all this was the product of a single mind or even of a generation; most likely the period of evolution and experimentation was simply not recorded by history.

After some initial battles while subjugating the Greeks of the Ionian coast, the Persians determined to invade Greece proper.

Themistocles of Athens estimated that the Greeks would be outnumbered by the Persians on land, but that Athens could protect itself by building a fleet (the famous "wooden walls"), using the profits of the silver mines at Laurium to finance them.

The first Persian campaign, in 492 BC, was aborted because the fleet was lost in a storm, but the second, in 490 BC, captured islands in the Aegean Sea before landing on the mainland near Marathon. Attacks by the Greek armies repulsed these.

The third Persian campaign, under Xerxes I of Persia ten years later (480 BC), followed the pattern of the first in marching the army via the Hellespont while the fleet paralleled them offshore. Near Artemisium, in the narrow channel between the mainland and Euboea, the Greek fleet held off multiple assaults by the Persians, the Persians breaking through a first line, but then being flanked by the second line of ships. But the defeat on land at Thermopylae forced a Greek withdrawal, and Athens evacuated its population to nearby Salamis Island.

The ensuing Battle of Salamis was one of the decisive engagements of history. Themistocles trapped the Persians in a channel too narrow for them to bring their greater numbers to bear, and attacked them vigorously, in the end causing the loss of 200 Persian ships vs 40 Greek. At the end, Xerxes still had a fleet stronger than the Greeks, but withdrew anyway, and after losing at Plataea in the following year, returned to Asia Minor, leaving the Greeks their freedom. Nevertheless, the Athenians and Spartans attacked and burned the laid-up Persian fleet at Mycale, and freed many of the Ionian towns.

During the next fifty years, the Greeks commanded the Aegean, but not harmoniously. After several minor wars about which we know little, tensions exploded into the Peloponnesian War (431 B.C.) between Athens' Delian League and the Spartan Peloponnese. Naval strategy was critical; Athens walled itself off from the rest of Greece, leaving only the port at Piraeus open, and trusting in its navy to keep supplies flowing while the Spartan army besieged it. This strategy worked, although the close quarters likely contributed to the plague that killed many Athenians in 429.

There were a number of sea battles between galleys; at Rhium, Naupactus, Pylos, Syracuse, Cynossema, Cyzicus, Notium. But the end came for Athens in 405 at Aegospotami in the Hellespont, where the Athenians had drawn up their fleet on the beach, and were surprised by the Spartan fleet, who landed and burned all the ships. Athens surrendered to Sparta in the following year. Navies next played a major role in the complicated wars of the successors of Alexander the Great.

The Roman Republic had never been much of a seafaring nation, but it had to learn, and learn fast, in the Punic Wars with Carthage, and developed the technique of grappling and boarding enemy ships with soldiers. The Roman Navy grew gradually as Rome found itself involved in more and more Mediterranean politics; by the time of the Roman Civil War and the Battle of Actium in 31 BC, hundreds of ships were involved, many of them quinqueremes mounting catapults and fighting towers. Following the Emperor Augustus transforming the Republic into the Roman Empire, Rome gained control of most of the Mediterranean. Without any significant maritime enemies, the Roman navy was reduced mostly to patroling for pirates and transportation duties. It was only on the fringes of the Empire, in newly gained provincies or defensive missions against barbarian invasion, did the navy still engage in actual warfare.

Ancient China

In ancient China, the first known naval battles took place during the Warring States (481 BC-221 BC), a period where regional kings battled against one another. Chinese naval warfare in this ancient period featured grapple-and-hook, as well as ramming tactics with ships called "stomach strikers" and "colliding swoopers". It was written in the subsequent Han Dynasty that the Warring States era Chinese had employed *ge chuan* ships (dagger-axe ships, or halberd ships), thought to have a simple description of a ship manned by marines carrying dagger-axe halberds as personal weapons. The later 3rd century Three Kingdoms era Chinese writer Zhang Yan asserted in his writing that the Warring States Chinese named the boats this way because halberd blades were actually fixed and attached to the hull of the ship in order to rip into the hull of another ship while ramming, to stab enemies in the water that had fallen overboard and were swimming, or simply to clear any possible dangerous marine animals in the path of the ship. Qin Shi Huang, the first emperor of the Qin Dynasty (221 BC-207 BC), owed much of his success in unifying China (specifically southern China) to naval power, although an official navy was not yet established. Zhou Dynasty era Chinese were known to use temporary pontoon bridges for general means of transportation, but it was during the Qin and later Han Dynasty that large permanent pontoon bridges were assembled, and used for purposes of warfare (first written account of a pontoon bridge in the West being the oversight of the Greek Mandrocles of Samos in aiding a military campaign of Persian Emperor Darius I over the Bosporus).

During the Han Dynasty (202 BC-AD 220), the Chinese discovered the use of the stern-mounted steering rudder, as well as designed a new ship type, the junk. During the late Han Dynasty into the Three Kingdoms period, significantly large naval battles like the Battle of Chibi marked the advancement of naval warfare in the East. In the latter engagement, the Chinese military strategist Zhuge Liang from the Kingdom of Shu is well known for his fire attack upon the massive naval fleet of Prime Minister Cao Cao.

In terms of seafaring abroad, arguably one of the first Chinese to sail into the Indian Ocean and to reach Sri Lanka and India by sea was the Buddhist monk Fa Xian in the early 5th century (although diplomatic ties and land trade to Persia and India was established during the earlier Han Dynasty). However, Chinese naval maritime influence would not present itself in the Indian Ocean until the medieval period.

Europe, Middle East and North Africa

The barbarian invasions of the 4th century and later mostly occurred by land, but there are mentions of a Vandal fleet fighting with the Romans, and a defeat of an Ostrogothic fleet at Sena Gallica in the Adriatic Sea. During the Muslim conquests of the 7th century, Arab fleets begin to make an appearance, raiding Sicily in 652, and defeating the Byzantine Navy in 655. Constantinople is saved from a prolonged Arab siege in 678 by the invention of Greek fire, an early form of flamethrower that was devastating to the ships in the besieging fleet. These were just the first of many encounters during the Byzantine-Arab Wars.

The Islamic Caliphate, or Arab Empire, became the dominant naval power in the Mediterranean Sea from the 7th to 13th centuries, during what is known as the Islamic Golden Age. One of the most significant inventions in medieval naval warfare was the torpedo, invented in Syria by the Arab inventor Hasan al-Rammah in 1275. His torpedo ran on water with a rocket system filled with explosive gunpowder materials and had three firing points. It was a very effective weapon against ships. In the 8th century the Norse Vikings begin to make an appearance, although their usual style is to appear quickly, plunder, and disappear, preferably undefended locations. King Alfred the Great of England built a fleet and was able to stay the Viking incursions, establishing the boundaries of Danelaw in a 884 treaty.

The Norse also fought several sea battles among themselves. This was normally done by binding the ships on each side together, thus essentially fighting a land battle on the sea. However the fact that the losing side could not easily escape meant that battles tended to be hard and bloody. The Battle of Svolder is perhaps the most famous of these battles.

As Arab power in the Mediterranean began to wane, the Italian trading towns of Genoa, Pisa, and Venice stepped in to seize the opportunity, setting up commercial networks and building navies to protect them. At first the navies fought with the Arabs (off Bari in 1004, at Messina in 1005), but then they found themselves contending with Normans moving into Sicily, and finally with each other. The Genoese and Venetians fought four naval wars, in 1253–1284, 1293–1299, 1350–1355, and 1378–1381. The last ended with a decisive victory for Venice, which gave them almost a century to enjoy Mediterranean trade domination before other European countries started exploring to the south and west.

In the north of Europe, the near-continuous conflict between England and France was characterised by a number of raids on coastal towns and ports along each other coastlines and the securing of sea lanes to protect transports carrying troops from England to France. The Battle of Dover in 1217, between a French fleet of 80 ships under Eustace the Monk and an English fleet of 40 under Hubert de Burgh, is notable as the first recorded battle using sailing ship tactics. The Battle of Sluys, fought in 1340, marked the opening of the Hundred Years War; the battle saw the desturuction of the French fleet in an action as decisive as Midway or Tsushima and allowed the English effective control of the sea lanes and the strategic initiative for much of the war.

East and South Asia

The Sui Dynasty (581-618) and Tang Dynasty (618-907) of China were involved in several naval affairs over the triple-set of polities ruling medieval Korea (Three Kingdoms of Korea), along with engaging naval bombardments on the peninsula from Asuka period Yamato Kingdom (Japan). A prominent factor in the sudden decline and collapse of the Sui Dynasty was its pouring of state funds into the Goguryeo-Sui Wars, where the Chinese assembled an enormous naval fleet that in the end was unsuccessful. The succeeding Tang Dynasty of China took on a different foreign policy, aiding the Silla Dynasty in expelling the armies and naval forces of the Japanese and conquering Silla's other Korean rivals, Baekje and Goguryeo by 668. In addition, the Chinese Tang Dynasty had maritime trading, tributary, and diplomatic ties as far as modern-day Sri Lanka, India, Islamic Iran and Arabia, as well as Somalia in East Africa.

From the Axumite Kingdom in modern-day Ethiopia, the Arab traveller Sa'd ibn Abi-Waqqas sailed from there to Tang China during the reign of Emperor Gaozong. Two decades later, he returned with a copy of the Quran, establishing the first Islamic mosque in China, the Mosque of Remembrance in Guangzhou. What followed was a rising rivalry between Arab and Chinese for dominant control of sea lanes of trade in the Indian Ocean. In his book *Cultural Flow Between China and the Outside World*, Shen Fuwei notes that maritime Chinese merchants in the 9th century were landing regularly at Sufala in East Africa to cut out Arab middle-men traders.

The Chola Dynasty of medieval India was a dominant seapower in the Indian Ocean, an avid maritime trader and diplomatic entity with Song China. Rajaraja Chola I (reigned 985 to 1014) and his son Rajendra Chola I (reigned 1014-42), who were from the Dravidian kingdom in southern India, sent out a great naval expedition that occupied parts of Myanmar, Malaya, and Sumatra. While many believe the Cholas were the first rulers noted to have a naval fleet in the Indian subcontinent, there are at least two evidences to cite use of navies. Narasimhavarman Pallava I transported his troops to Sri Lanka to help Manavarman to reclaim the throne. Shatavahanahas were known to possess a navy that was widely deployed to influence Southeast Asia. What is not known is the extent of use. Some argue that there is no evidence to support naval warfare in a contemporary sense. Others say that ships routinely carried bands of archers to keep pirates at bay. However, since the Arabs were known to use catapults, naptha, and devices attached to ships to prevent boarding parties, one can reasonably conclude that Chola navies not only transported troops but also provided support, protection, and attack capabilities against enemy targets

12TH CENTURY

In the 12th century, China's first permanent standing navy was established by the Southern Song Dynasty, the headquarters of the Admiralty stationed at Ding-hai. This came about after the conquest of northern China by the Jurchen people in 1127, while the Chinese court fled south from Kaifeng to Hangzhou. Equipped with the magnetic compass and knowledge of Shen Kuo's famous treatise (on the concept of true north), the Chinese became proficient experts of navigation in their day. They raised their naval strength from a mere 11 squadrons of 3,000 marines to 20 squadrons of 52,000 marines in a century's time.

Employing paddle wheel crafts and trebuchet's throwing gunpowder bombs from the decks of their ships, the Chinese became a formidable foe to the Jin Dynasty during the 12th-13th centuries. With a powerful navy, China dominated maritime trade throughout South East Asia as well. Until 1279, the Chinese were able to use their naval power to defend against the Jin to the north, until the Mongols finally conquered all of China. After the Song Dynasty, the Mongol-led Yuan Dynasty of China was a powerful maritime force in the Indian Ocean. The Yuan Emperor Kublai Khan attempted to invade Japan twice with enormous fleets (of both Mongols and Chinese), in 1274 and again in 1281, both attempts being unsuccessful. Building upon the technological achievements of the earlier Chinese Song Dynasty, the Mongols also employed early cannons upon the decks of their ships.

While the Chinese Song Dynasty built its naval strength, the Japanese also had considerable naval prowess. The strength of Japanese naval forces could be seen in the Genpei War, in the large-scale Battle of Dan-no-ura on April 25, 1185. The forces of Minamoto no Yoshitsune were 850 ships strong, while Taira no Munemori had 500 ships under his command. In the mid 14th century, the rebel leader Zhu Yuanzhang (1328-1398) seized power in the south amongst many other rebel groups. His early success was owed to the aid of capable officials such as Liu Ji and Jiao Yu, and their gunpowder weapons. Yet the decisive battle that cemented his success and his founding of the Ming Dynasty (1368-1644) was the Battle of Lake Poyang, considered one of the largest naval battles in history.

In the 15th century, the Chinese Ming Dynasty Admiral Zheng He was assigned to assemble a massive fleet for several tributary missions abroad, sailing throughout the waters of the South East Pacific and the Indian Ocean. During his maritime missions, on several occasions Zheng's fleet came into conflict with pirates. Zheng's fleet also became involved in a conflict in Sri Lanka, where the King of Ceylon travelled back to Ming China afterwards to make a formal apology to the Emperor.

In the late 16th century, Toyotomi Hideyoshi of Momoyama-era Japan gathered an enormous fleet to assault the Joseon Dynasty of Korea when the Korean King Seonjo refused to allow Japanese armies to invade Ming Dynasty China via the Korean Peninsula as a staging ground. During the Japanese invasions of Korea (1592-1598), the Japanese employed clever close-range tactics on land with arquebus rifles, but also relied upon close-range firing of muskets in grapple-and-board style naval engagements.

The Japanese were successful in first capturing the Korean port at Busan, the capital at Hanseong (In modern-day Seoul) fell to their forces, and then proceeded to move far north into the Korean peninsula. Military aid sent by Chinese Wanli Emperor of Ming assisted the Koreans somewhat, but the farther firing range of Korean cannons, along with the brilliant naval strategies of the Korean Admiral Yi Sun-sin, were the main detrimental factors in ultimate Japanese defeats. Admiral Yi is credited Turtle ship (Geobukseon). Turtle Ships were used mostly to spearhead attacks. They were best used in tight areas and around islands rather than the open sea. Admiral Yi effectively cut off the possible Japanese supply line that would have run through the Yellow Sea to China, as well as severely weakened the Japanese strength and fighting morale in several heated engagements (where many regard the most critical Japanese defeat to be the Battle of Hansan Island).

Sails and Empires

The early 17th century galleon *Vasa.* on display at the Vasa Museum in Stockholm. *Vasa,* with its high stern castle and double battery decks, was a transitional design between the preferences for boarding tactics and the line of battle. The late Middle Ages was important as the time of the development of the cogs, caravels and carracks ships capable of surviving the tough conditions of the open ocean, with enough backup systems and crew expertise to make long voyages routine. In addition, they grew from 100 tons to 300 tons displacement, enough to carry cannons as armament and still have space left over for profitable cargo. One of the largest ships of the time, the Great Harry displaced over 1,500 tons.

The voyages of discovery were fundamentally commercial rather than military in nature, although the line was sometimes blurry in that a country's ruler was not above funding exploration for personal profit, nor was it a problem to use military power to enhance that profit. Later the lines gradually separated, in that the ruler's motivation in using the navy was to protect private enterprise so that they could pay more taxes.

Like the Egyptian Shia-Fatimids and Mamluks, the Sunni-Islamic Ottoman Empire centred in modern-day Turkey dominated the eastern Mediterranean Sea. The Ottomans built a powerful navy, rivaling the Italian city-state of Venice during the Ottoman-Venetian Wars (1499-1503). Although they were sorely defeated in the Battle of Lepanto (1571) by the Holy League, the Ottomans quickly rebuilt their naval strength, and afterwards successfully defended the island of Cyprus so that it would stay in Ottoman hands. However, with the concurrent Age of Discovery, Europe had far surpassed the Ottoman Empire, and successfully bypassed their reliance on land-trade by discovering maritime routes around Africa and towards the Americas.

The first naval action in defence of the new colonies was just ten years after Vasco da Gama's epochal landing in India. In March 1508, a combined Gujarati/Egyptian force surprised a Portuguese squadron at Dabul, and only two Portuguese ships escaped. The following February, the Portuguese viceroy destroyed the allied fleet at Battle of Diu, thus confirming Portuguese domination of the Indian Ocean. In 1582, the Battle of Ponta Delgada in the Azores, in which a Spanish fleet defeated a combined Portuguese, French, English and Dutch force, thus suppressing a revolt in the islands, was the first battle fought in mid-Atlantic.

In 1588, Philip II of Spain sent his Spanish Armada to subdue Elizabeth I of England, but Admiral Sir Charles Howard forced its retreat, beginning the rise to prominence of the Royal Navy. However it was unable to follow up with a decisive blow against the Spanish navy, which remained the most important for another half century. After the war's end in 1604 the English fleet went through a time of relative neglect and decline. In the 16th century, the Barbary Coast | Barbary states of North Africa rose to power and they collectively became a dominant naval power in the Mediterranean Sea due to the Barbary pirates. The coastal villages and towns of Italy, Spain and List of islands in the Mediterranean | Mediterranean islands were frequently attacked by them and long stretches of the Italian and Spanish coasts were almost completely abandoned by their inhabitants; after 1600 Barbary pirates occasionally entered the Atlantic and struck as far north as Iceland.

According to Robert Davis between 1 million and 1.25 million Europeans were captured by Barbary pirates and sold as slaves in North Africa and the Ottoman Empire between the 16th and 19th centuries. These slaves were captured mainly from seaside villages in Italy, Spain and Portugal, and from farther places like France, England, the Netherlands, Ireland and even Iceland and North America. The Barbary pirates were also able to successfully defeat and capture many European ships, which was largely due to advances in sailing technology by the Barbary states. The earliest naval trawler, xebec and windward ships were employed by the Barbary pirates from the 16th century.

From the middle of the 17th century competition between the expanding English and Dutch commercial fleets came to a head in the Anglo-Dutch Wars, the first wars to be conducted entirely at sea. Most memorable of these battles was the raid on the Medway, in which the Dutch admiral Michiel de Ruyter sailed up the river Thames, and destroyed most of the British fleet. This remains to date the greatest naval defeat of England and her consecutive countries, and established Dutch supremacy at sea for over half a century. The English and Dutch wars were also known for very few ships being sunk, as it was very difficult to hit ships below the water level; the water surface deflected cannon balls, and the few holes produced could be patched quickly. Naval forces were severely weakened by casualties to the men and damage to the sails more than by loss of ships.

The 18th century developed into a period of seemingly continuous world wars, each larger than the last. At sea, the British and French were bitter rivals; the French aided the fledgling United States in the American Revolutionary War, but their strategic purpose was to capture territory in India and the West Indies—which they did not achieve.

In the Baltic Sea, the final attempt to revive the Swedish Empire led to Gustav III's Russian War, with its grande finale at the Second Battle of Svensksund. The battle was unrivalled in size until the 20th century, was a decisive Swedish tactical victory but its strategical result was poor (due to poor army performance and previous lack of initiative from the Swedes) and the war ended without any territorial changes.

Even the change of government due to the French Revolution seemed to intensify rather than diminish the rivalry, and the Napoleonic Wars included a series of legendary naval battles, culminating in the Battle of Trafalgar in 1805, by which Admiral Horatio Nelson broke the power of the French and Spanish fleets, but lost his own life in so doing.

From Wood and Wind to Steel and Steam

Trafalgar ushered in the *Pax Britannica* of the 19th century, marked by general peace in the world's oceans, under the ensigns of the Royal Navy. But the period was one of intensive experimentation with new technology; steam power for ships appeared in the 1810s, improved metallurgy and machining technique produced larger and deadlier guns, and the development of explosive shells, capable of demolishing a wooden ship at a single blow, in turn required the addition of iron armour.

Although naval power during the Song, Yuan, and Ming dynasties established China as a major world seapower in the East, the Qing Dynasty lacked an official standing navy. They were more interested in pouring funds into military ventures closer to home (China proper), such as Mongolia, Tibet, and Central Asia (modern Xinjiang). However, there were some considerable naval conflicts during the Qing Dynasty before the Opium Wars (such as the Battle of Penghu, or the conflict against Koxinga).

The insignificant naval effort that the Manchus/Chinese pitted against the more advanced British steam-powered ships during the first of the Opium Wars in the 1840s was sorely defeated. This left China open to virtual foreign domination (from European powers and then Japan) via spheres of influence over regions of China for economic gain. Although the Qing Dynasty attempted to modernize the Chinese navy, China's Beiyang Fleet was dealt a severe blow by the Imperial Japanese Navy in the First Sino-Japanese War (1894-1895).

The famous battle of the CSS *Virginia* and USS *Monitor* in the American Civil War was the duel of ironclads that symbolized the changing times. The first fleet action between ironclad ships was fought in 1866 at the Battle of Lissa between the navies of Austria and Italy. Because the decisive moment of the battle occurred when the Austrian flagship the *Erzherzog Ferdinand Max* successfully sank the Italian flagship *Re d'Italia* by ramming, in subsequent decades every navy in the world largely focused on ramming as the main tactic. As the century came to a close, the familiar modern battleship began to emerge; a steel-armored ship, entirely dependent on steam, and sporting a number of large shell guns mounted in turrets arranged along the centerline of the main deck. The ultimate design was reached in 1906 with the *HMS Dreadnought (1906)* which entirely dispensed with smaller guns, her main guns being sufficient to sink any existing ship of the time.

The Russo-Japanese War and particularly the Battle of Tsushima in 1905 was the first test of the new concepts, resulting a stunning Japanese victory and the destruction of most Russian ships. With the advent of the steamship, it became possible to create massive gun platforms and to provide them with heavy armour protection. The Dreadnought battleships and their successors were the first capital ships that combined technology and firepower with a mobile platform. However, in the first half of the 20th century, the utility of air power in support of the fleet began to emerge;

World War I pitted the old Royal Navy against the new navy of Imperial Germany, culminating in the 1916 Battle of Jutland. The future was heralded when the seaplane carrier HMS *Engadine* and her Short 184 sea planes joined the battle. Meanwhile, in the Black Sea, Russian seaplanes flying from a fleet of converted carriers interdicted Turkish maritime supply routes, Allied air patrols began to counter German U-Boat activity in Britain's coastal waters, and a British Short 184 seplane carried out the first successful torpedo attack ona ship.

In 1918 the Royal Navy converted an Italian liner to create the first aircraft carrier, HMS *Argus*, and shotrtly after the war the first purpose-built carrier, HMS Hermes was launched. Many nations agreed to the Washington Naval Treaty and scrapped many of their battleships and cruisers while still in the shipyards, but the growing tensions of the 1930s restarted the building programs, with even larger ships than before; *Yamato*, the largest battleship ever, displaced 72,000 tons and mounted 18.1-inch (460 mm) guns.

Above and Below the Surface

The victory of the Royal Navy at the Battle of Taranto was a pivotal point as this was the first true demonstration of naval air power. Following 7 December 1941 when the United States came into World War II, the sinking of HMS Prince of Wales and HMS Repulse marked the end of the era of the battleship, and the new importance of aircraft and their transportation, the aircraft carrier, came to the fore. During the Pacific War, battleships and cruisers spent most of their time bombarding shore positions, while the carriers were the stars of the key Battle of the Coral Sea, Battle of Midway, Battle of the Philippine Sea, and the climactic Battle of Leyte Gulf. Air power remained key to navies throughout the 20th century, moving to jets launched from ever-larger carriers, and augmented by cruisers armed with guided missiles and cruise missiles.

Roughly parallel to the development of naval aviation was the development of submarines to travel underneath the sea, at first for short dives, then later to be able to spend weeks or months underwater powered by a nuclear reactor. In both World Wars, submarines (U-boats in Germany) primarily exerted their power by using torpedoes to sink merchant ships, as well as other warships. In the 1950s the Cold War inspired the development of ballistic missile submarines, each one loaded with dozens of nuclear-armed missiles and with orders to launch them from sea should the other nation attack. Against the backdrop of these developments, World War II had seen the United States become by far the largest Naval power in the world. Throughout the rest of the 20th century The United States Navy would maintain a tonnage greater than that of the next 17 largest navies combined.

The only major naval conflict that took place in the second half of the 20th century was the well known Falklands War, pitting Argentina against the United Kingdom. The Falklands showed the vulnerability of modern ships to sea-skimming missiles like the Exocet. One hit from an Exocet sank HMS *Sheffield*, a modern anti-air warfare destroyer. Important lessons about ship design, damage control and ship construction materials were learnt from the conflict.

At the present time, large naval wars seem to be very rare affairs, with the main function of the modern navy being to exploit its control of the seaways to project power ashore. Power projection has been the primary naval feature of conflicts like the Korean War, Suez Crisis, Vietnam War, Konfrontasi, Gulf War, Kosovo War and both campaigns of the War on Terrorism in Afghanistan and Iraq.

NAVAL STRATEGY

Naval strategy, and the related concept of maritime strategy, concerns the overall strategy for achieving victory at sea, including the planning and conduct of campaigns, the movement and disposition of naval forces by which a commander secures the advantage of fighting at a place convenient to himself, and the deception of the enemy. Naval tactics deal with the execution of plans and manœuvering of ships or fleets in battle.

PRINCIPLES OF NAVAL STRATEGY

The great aims of a fleet in war must be to keep the coast of its own country free from attack, to secure the freedom of its trade, and to destroy the enemy's fleet or confine it to port. The first and second of these aims can be attained by the successful achievement of the third – the destruction or paralysis of the hostile fleet. A fleet that secures the freedom of its own communications from attack is said to have command of the sea. Naval strategy is fundamentally different from military strategy. At sea there is no territory to occupy. Apart from the fisheries and, more recently, offshore oilfields, there are no economic assets that can be denied to the enemy and no resources that a fleet can exploit. While an army can live off the land, a fleet must rely on whatever supplies it carries with it or can be brought to it.

THE EVOLUTION OF NAVAL STRATEGY

Torrington and the Fleet in Being

The Earl of Torrington is credited with being the first to use the expression, *fleet in being*. Faced with a clearly superior French fleet in the summer of 1690, Torrington proposed avoiding battle, except under very favourable conditions, until the arrival of reinforcements. By maintaining his fleet *in being*, he would prevent the French from gaining command of the sea, which would allow them to invade England. Although Torrington was forced to fight at the Battle of Beachy Head, the defeat was not enough to give the French command of the sea.

Introduction of the Guerre de Course

By the mid 1690s, privateers from French Atlantic ports,

particularly St. Malo and Dunkirk, were a major threat to Anglo-Dutch commerce. The threat forced the English government to divert warships to the defence of trade, as convoy escorts and cruisers to hunt down the privateers. In France, the success of privateers against the Anglo-Dutch war effort stimulated a gradual shift from the employment of the Royal warships as battlefleets (*guerre d'esquadron*) towards supporting the war on trade (*guerre de course*). The allied convoys presented large targets for commerce raiding squadrons. The most dramatic result of this shift was the Comte de Tourville's attack upon the allies' Smyrna convoy on 17 June 1693.

The disadvantage of the *guerre de course* when pursued as a battlefleet strategy, rather than just by smaller vessels, is that it leaves a country's own trade defenceless. Individual raiding squadrons are also vulnerable to defeat in detail if the enemy sends larger squadrons in pursuit, as happened to Leissegues at the Battle of San Domingo in 1806 and Von Spee at the Battle of the Falkland Islands in 1914.

Hawke, St Vincent and the Close Blockade

Until after the end of the 17th century it was thought impossible, or at least very rash, to keep the great ships out of port between September and May or June. Therefore continuous watch on an enemy by blockading his ports was beyond the power of any navy. Therefore too, as an enemy fleet might be at sea before it could be stopped, the movements of fleets were much subordinated to the need for providing convoy to the trade.

It was not until the middle of the 18th century that the continuous blockade first carried out by Sir Edward Hawke in 1758–59, and then brought to perfection by Earl St Vincent and other British admirals between 1793 and 1815, became possible.

Mahan, Corbett and the development of theory

It was only at the very end of the 19th century that theories of naval strategy were first codified, even though British statesmen and admirals had been practising it for centuries.

Mahan's influence on strategy

Captain, later Rear-Admiral, Alfred Thayer Mahan (1840-

1914) was an American naval officer and historian. Influenced by Jomini's principles of strategy, he argued that in the coming wars, control of the sea would grant the power to control the trade and resources needed to wage war. Mahan's premise was that in the contests between France and Britain in the 18th century, domination of the sea through naval power was the deciding factor in the outcome, and therefore, that control of seaborne commerce was critical to domination in war. In Mahan's view, a country obtained "command of the sea" by concentrating its naval forces at the decisive point to destroy or master the enemy's battle fleet; blockade of enemy ports and disruption of the enemy's maritime communications would follow. Mahan believed that the true objective in a naval war was always the enemy fleet.

Mahan's writings were highly influential. His best-known books, *The Influence of Sea Power upon History, 1660-1783*, and *The Influence of Sea Power upon the French Revolution and Empire, 1793-1812*, were published in 1890 and 1892 respectively and his theories contributed to the naval arms race between 1898 and 1914.

The Colomb Brothers and Naval Warfare

In Britain, Captain John H. Colomb (1838-1909) in a series of articles and lectures argued that the navy was the most important component of imperial defence; his brother, Admiral Phillip Colomb (1831-1899), sought to establish from history general rules applicable to modern naval warfare in his *Naval Warfare* (1891). But their writings achieved nothing like the fame achieved by Mahan.

Corbett's Principles of Maritime Strategy

Sir Julian Corbett (1854-1922) was a British naval historian who became a lecturer at the Royal Naval War College in Great Britain.

Corbett differed from Mahan in placing much less emphasis on fleet battle. Corbett emphasized the interdependence of naval and land warfare and tended to concentrate on the importance of sea communications rather than battle. Battle at sea was not an end in itself; the primary objective of the fleet was to secure one's own communications and disrupt those of the enemy, not necessarily to seek out and destroy the enemy's fleet. To Corbett, command of the sea was a relative and not an absolute which could be categorized as general or local, temporary or permanent. Corbett defined the two fundamental methods of obtaining control of the lines of communication as the actual physical destruction or capture of enemy warships and merchants, and or a naval blockade. His most famous work, *Some Principles of Maritime Strategy*, remains a classic.

THE IMPACT OF THE WORLD WARS

The submarine, introduced in World War I, led to the development of new weapons and tactics. In both world wars the submarine was employed mainly as a commerce destroyer and, as such, could not by itself gain command of the sea. But the *guerre de course* in the form of the submarine campaign almost defeated the British in 1917, until the belated reintroduction of convoy. The same strategy, deployed by the Americans, overwhelmed Japan in the Pacific from 1943 onwards. Similar German efforts to interrupt Allied trade with surface warships and auxiliaries operating as commerce destroyers on the trade routes caused great disruption and delay, but never truly threatened Allied communications in either war. The development of air power led to further tactical changes, including the emergence of aircraft carriers and naval air fleets. Rather than invade every Japanese-held island in the Pacific, the Americans developed the island-hopping strategy of neutralizing and then bypassing the major Japanese bases, only taking the islands needed to provide bases for the fleet or air forces. By the end of the Second World War, it was clear that command of the sea rested not just on control of the surface of the sea, but also the air above it and the waters beneath it.

MODERN NAVAL STRATEGY

Increasingly naval strategy has been merged with general strategy involving land and air warfare. Naval strategy constantly evolves as improved technologies become available. During the Cold War, for example, the Soviet Navy shifted from a strategy of directly contending against NATO for control of the bluewater oceans to a concentrated defence of the Barents Sea and the Sea of Okhotsk bastions. In 2007, the U.S. Navy joined with the U.S. Marine Corps and U.S. Coast Guard to adopt a new maritime strategy called A Cooperative Strategy for 21st Century Seapower that raised the notion of prevention of war to the same philosophical level as the conduct of war. The strategy was presented by the Chief of Naval Operations, the Commandant of the Marine Corps and Commandant of the Coast Guard at the International Seapower Symposium in Newport, R.I.. The strategy recognized the economic links of the global system and how any disruption due to regional crises – manmade or natural – can adversely impact the U.S. economy and quality of life. This new strategy charted a course for the three U.S. sea services to work collectively with each other and international partners to prevent these crises from occurring or reacting quickly should one occur to avoid negative impacts to the United States.

COMMAND OF THE SEA

A naval force has command of the sea when it is so strong that its rivals cannot attack it directly. Also called sea control, this dominance may apply to its surrounding waters (i.e., the littoral) or may extend far into the oceans, meaning the country has a blue-water navy. It is the naval equivalent of air superiority. With command of the sea, a country (or alliance) can ensure that its own military and merchant ships can move around at will, while its rivals are forced either to stay in port or to try to evade it.

Most famously, the British Royal Navy held command of the sea for long periods from the 18th to the early 20th century, allowing Britain and its allies to trade and to move troops and supplies easily in wartime while its enemies could not (the importance of which is reflected in the famous British patriotic song, "Rule, Britannia!," which contains the exhortation, "Rule Britannia! Britannia rule the waves", even if this was not the poem's original subject). For example, Britain was able to blockade France during the Napoleonic Wars, the United States during the War of 1812, and Germany during World War I.

Few navies can operate as blue-water navies, but "many States are converting green-water navies to blue-water navies and this will increase military use of foreign Exclusive Economic Zones [littoral zone to 200 nautical miles (370 km)] with possible repercussions for the EEZ regime."

Legal Context

Gradually, however, countries agreed that the open seas should be free to all shipping in peacetime and to neutral shipping in wartime. Great Britain accepted the principle in 1805; Russia, in 1824; and the United States (tacitly) in 1894. Many treaties, including the Treaty of Versailles, have dealt with the open seas, and currently the United Nations Convention on the Law of the Sea formalizes this freedom.

HISTORIC COMMAND OF THE SEA DURING THE AGE OF SAIL

National Capabilities

Historically, many powers attempted to extend command of the sea into peacetime, imposing taxes or other restrictions on shipping using areas of open sea. For example, Venice claimed the Adriatic, and exacted a heavy toll from vessels navigating its northern waters. Genoa and France each claimed portions of the western Mediterranean. Denmark and Sweden claimed to share the Baltic between them. Spain claimed dominion over the Pacific and the Gulf of Mexico, and Portugal over the Indian Ocean and all the Atlantic south of Morocco (Hall, 148-9).

Asymmetric Countermeasures

During the age of sail, there were two primary counter measures to another power holding control of the sea: smuggling, and privateering. Smuggling helped to ensure that a country could continue trading (and obtaining food and other vital supplies) even when under blockade, while privateering allowed the weaker power to disrupt the stronger power's trade. As these measures, which are examples of asymmetric warfare, came from non-governmental and sometimes criminal organizations, they fell into disfavor with stronger governments. An annex to the Treaty of Paris (1856) banned privateering. That treaty was an oddity in that it was ratified by relatively few countries, but quickly became the *de facto* law of the sea.

Historic Command of the Sea in the Era of Steam

A more modern countermeasure, similar to privateering, was the use of submarine warfare by Germany during World War I and World War II to attack allied merchant shipping primarily in the Atlantic Ocean, Mediterranean Sea, and Baltic Sea. During World War II, aircraft also became an effective countermeasure to command of the sea, since ships could not defend themselves well against air attack. The Battle of Britain was largely an attempt by Germany to eliminate the Royal Air Force, so that it would not be able to defend the Royal Navy from air attack and even to allow a maritime invasion of Great Britain proper.

Modern Command of the Sea

Advanced navies, with access to surveillance satellites and large-scale submarine detection systems, can rarely be surprised at sea, but cannot be everywhere. Individual ships of advanced navies can be vulnerable at sea (e.g., the USS *Stark* hit by an aircraft-delivered antiship missile while patrolling the Persian Gulf) or in port (e.g., by the suicide attack on the USS *Cole*.)

"Blue-water" (high seas) naval capability means that a fleet is able to operate on the "high seas." While traditionally a distinction was made between the coastal brown-water navy (operating in the littoral zone to 200 nautical miles (370 km) and a seagoing blue-water navy, a new term, "green-water navy," has been created by the U.S. Navy, which refers to the coastal submarines and fast attack boats of many nations, the larger littoral combat corvettes and similar vessels of a substantial number of powers, and amphibious vessels ranging from elderly LSTs to complex S/VTOL carriers and other specialized ships. The term *brown-water navy* appears to have been reduced, in U.S. Navy parlance, to a riverine force. In modern warfare blue-water navy implies self-contained force protection from sub-surface, surface and airborne threats and a sustainable logistic reach, allowing a persistent presence at range. In some maritime environments such a defence is given by natural obstacles, such as the Arctic ice shelf.

Requirements for Modern Sea Control

During the Falklands War, the British lacked long-range

Airborne Warning and Control System (AWACS), which led to ship losses and major damage to others, when the Argentinian attack aircraft came into the view of ship radar at approximately the same time they would fire antiship missiles, and only a short time before they made bombing attacks. A number of navies have learned this lesson. Navies with STOVL carriers have developed helicopter-mounted AWACS like the British and Spanish Westland Sea King AEW, Italian EH-101 AEW, and the Russian Ka-31 AEW helicopter. Recently the French with a new larger CATOBAR aircraft carrier obtained the US E-2 Hawkeye AWACS aircraft.

An example for the difference between a blue-water navy and a green-water navy: "...The first should be a 'green-water active defence' that would enable the People's Liberation Army Navy to protect China's territorial waters and enforce its sovereignty claims in the Taiwan Strait and the South China Sea. The second phase would be to develop a blue-water navy capable of projecting power into the western Pacific... Liu commander in chief of the PLAN 1982-88 and vice chairman of the Central Military Commission 1989-97] believed that in order to fulfill a blue-water capability, the PLAN had to obtain aircraft carriers..." Aircraft carriers are deployed with other specialized vessels in carrier battle groups, providing protection against sub-surface, surface and airborne threats.

As there is no clear definition of a blue-water navy, the status is disputed. Usually it is considered to be strongly linked to the maintenance of aircraft carriers capable of operating in the oceans. "In the early 80s there was a bitter and very public battle fought over whether or not to replace Australia's last aircraft carrier, HMAS *Melbourne*. Senior navy personnel warned without a carrier, Australia would be vulnerable to all types of threat. One ex-Chief of Navy went so far as to claim that we" (the Australians) "would no longer have a blue-water navy (one capable of operating away from friendly coasts)."

Countermeasures to Imposed Command

While a *blue-water navy* can project sea control power into another nation's littoral, it remains susceptible to threats from less capable forces. Sustainment and logistics at range yield high costs and there may be a saturation advantage over a deployed force through the use of land-based air or surface-to-surface missile assets, diesel-electric submarines, or asymmetric tactics such as Fast Inshore Attack Craft. An example of this vulnerability was the October 2000 USS *Cole* bombing in Aden. Definitions of terminology is the key to the application of the Law of the Sea. Definitions of a term can be determined from its generic characteristics and specific differences. Using this method, military hydrographic surveys are not a threat of use of forc

Terminology is of fundamental importance in the application of the Law of the Sea. During the Tokyo meeting most participants were of the opinion that the 1982 UNCLOS in establishing the EEZ left many terms undefined, and thus the regime ambiguous, particularly regarding military uses of foreign EEZs. This ambiguity is in turn reflected in national laws.

In Russian law, it is generally assumed that the definition of a term can be determined from its generic characteristics (*genus proximum*) and specific differences (*differentia specifica*) of the phenomenon being defined In this context, a generic feature distinguishing military activity from other activities is its purpose of ensuring the security of the flag State, and a specific difference is the use of weapons for such purposes.

Peaceful Uses

A well-known Eastern saying goes 'you may repeat a countless number of times the word halva, but it won't become sweeter in your mouth'. Imagine yourself as a captain of an antisubmarine cruiser instructing your crew to sail with 'peaceful purposes,' and that the activities on the cruise must be innocent and 'not prejudicial to the peace, good order or security of the coastal state' Every cruise of a naval vessel is related to training the crew in warfare. And any military vessel or aircraft can inflict damage on its opponents. If that possibility is taken at face value, then it would be necessary to ban all military activity outside the territory of the flag State.

Although the term 'peaceful uses' appears in official government statements and multilateral treaties before the 1982 UNCLOS, examination of State practice leads to the conclusion that this term still lacks an authoritative definition. However, 'peaceful' does not necessarily mean 'non-military'. Let us look at one of its early uses, in the Outer Space Treaty of 1967. The UN General Assembly resolution 1148 (XII) first introduced the phrase 'exclusively for peaceful purposes,' at the end of the 13th UN General Assembly meeting in 1958. In the debate, nearly all States used the term 'peaceful' as opposed to 'military'. Therefore, the common understanding was to avoid any military uses whatsoever. But at the time of the debate, both the United States and the Soviet Union were developing satellites to serve military objectives. When this became evident, the legal meaning of the phrase 'peaceful uses' changed from non-military to 'non-aggressive.' Accordingly, all military uses of outer space were permitted and lawful as long as they remained 'non-aggressive.'

Under the 1969 *Vienna Convention on the Law of Treaties*, the words in a treaty must be interpreted in accordance with their ordinary meaning. However, Article 31 of the Vienna Convention provides that in the process of interpretation any subsequent practice in the application of the treaty shall also be taken into account. Bearing in mind that the 1982 UNCLOS permits military activities except those explicitly prohibited by treaty or customary law, the term peaceful as applied to military uses in the EEZ should be understood as 'non-offensive...or without threat.' However, the regime of the EEZ is not static. Many States are converting green water navies to blue water navies and this will increase military use of foreign EEZs, with possible repercussions for the EEZ regime.

THREAT OF FORCE

It is true that the UN Charter uses the terms 'threats to the peace' and 'the threat or use of force.' But these terms are not defined in absolute terms but in relation to 'the territorial integrity or political independence of any state, or in any other manner inconsistent with the purposes of the United Nations' But there is no generally accepted meaning of 'threat' with respect to the EEZ. The etymology of the term equates it with a 'promise to cause harm or evil'. From a legal viewpoint it may be determined as 'arising from danger to cause physical, material or other damage to the State (and so to public interests, as well as to separate persons or interests thereof) in the maritime space of its EEZ.' Since the EEZ is established for protection of the coastal State's natural resources, the 'threat' or danger should be viewed as pertaining strictly to economic issues.

A commonality of threat and danger is that they both may cause damage to the economic security of the coastal State. But they are not the same. First, threat is different from danger by the degree of its readiness to cause damage. A threat is a stage of extreme aggravation of contradictions, an immediate pre-conflict state at which there is a readiness of any of the actors to use force with respect to another for attaining its purpose. Danger is the stage when contradictions are nascent, when one of the actors has the potential to use force or a threat of force in its interests, but is not yet ready to use it. Second, a threat includes two components: intent and opportunity to cause damage to security interests, while danger is limited to only one of these components. Third, a threat is always personified, and has a targeted nature implying the presence of an obvious source of the threat and an object of the threat. Unlike a threat, danger is often hypothetical, and its subject and/or object are unclear. Fourth, a danger comprises a potential threat to cause damage to security interests, but its application requires the relevant conditions (accumulation of opportunities and formation of intent). A threat is a direct opportunity to cause damage, separated from doing so only by the time necessary to decide to do so.

Thus a threat to a State's interests in its EEZ is readiness (intent plus opportunity) of one of the subjects (for instance, a military vessel) to cause damage to the sovereign rights of another subject (for instance, the coastal State) in order to resolve differences between them.

China considers 'military hydrographic survey' activities in the EEZ without the coastal State's permission as 'in a military sense, a type of battlefield preparation, and thus a threat of force against that State' Let us evaluate the use of force on the part of the coastal State in this case. 'Use of force' in the EEZ means the unlawful actions of a ship, aircraft or other means of a foreign State which violates the immunity of a military vessel or aircraft or other object of another State, including civilian ships and installations or structures owned by the State (and operated for non-commercial purposes), thus denying the right of the state to the freedom of the high seas, including physical impact on the ship, aircraft, other said objects or their crew. 'A threat to use force' means the threat to undertake the above. It would not appear as if normal military hydrographic surveys are a threat of use of force.

The term 'hostile intent' does not appear in the 1982 UNCLOS. However, navigation of military vessels or aircraft across the path of the coastal State's vessels or aircraft or the carrying out of close observation or simulated attack are recognized by the Russia–China Incidents Agreement as dangerous maneuvering which should be preceded by special signals. When a hostile act occurs, naval forces may use force, including armed force, proportionally, in self-defence for protection, neutralization or, if necessary, destruction of the threat.

Conclusions

Interpretation of a single word or term can be argued ad infinitum. Even when definitions are 'clarified' and 'exact', loopholes and differing perspectives always arise. Regarding the disagreements on terms describing the EEZ regime for foreign naval activity, many aspects are based on the different abilities to use naval power. As an example, the island state of Kiribati is composed of 33 small islands with a total area of 280.24 square miles. Twenty of these islands are inhabited by the nation's population of slightly less than 100,000. Kiribati's EEZ extends over 1,370,300 square miles of ocean, an astounding 4890 times its own land area. This is the equivalent of more than one-third the land area of the United States and about 25% of the EEZ area controlled by the United States. Kiribati does not have the military ability to control foreign naval activity in its EEZ. So it may well be tempted to use international law to create a regime in its favour. 'Due regard' is the 1982 UNCLOS key to reaching a balance.

3

Submarine Warfare

A submarine is a watercraft capable of independent operation below the surface of the water. It differs from a submersible, which has only limited underwater capability. The term submarine most commonly refers to large crewed autonomous vessels; however, historically or more casually, submarine can also refer to medium sized or smaller vessels (midget submarines, wet subs), Remotely Operated Vehicles or robots. The word submarine was originally an adjective meaning "under the sea", and so consequently other uses such as "submarine engineering" or "submarine cable" may not actually refer to submarines at all. Submarine was shortened from the term "submarine boat", and is often further shortened to "sub".

Submarines are referred to as "boats", regardless of their size, for historical reasons because vessels deployed from a ship are referred to as boats. The first submarines were launched in such a manner. The English term *U-boat* for a German submarine comes from the German word for submarine, *U-Boot*, itself an abbreviation for *Unterseeboot* ("undersea boat").

Although experimental submarines had been built before, submarine design took off during the 19th century. Submarines were first widely used in World War I, and feature in many large navies. Military usage ranges from attacking enemy ships or submarines, aircraft carrier protection, blockade running, ballistic missile submarines as part of a nuclear strike force, reconnaissance, conventional land attack (for example using a cruise missile), and covert insertion of special forces. Civilian uses for submarines include marine science, salvage, exploration and facility inspection/maintenance. Submarines can also be specialized to a function such as search and rescue, or undersea cable repair. Submarines are also used in tourism and for academic research.

Submarines have one of the largest ranges of capabilities in any vessel, ranging from small autonomous examples to one or two-person vessels operating for a few hours, to vessels which can remain submerged for 6 months such as the Russian Typhoon class. Submarines can work at greater depths than are survivable or practical for human divers. Modern deep diving submarines are derived from the bathyscaphe, which in turn was an evolution of the diving bell.

Most large submarines comprise a cylindrical body with hemispherical (and/or conical) ends and a vertical structure, usually located amidships, which houses communications and sensing devices as well as periscopes. In modern submarines this structure is the "sail" in American usage ("fin" in European usage). A "conning tower" was a feature of earlier designs: a separate pressure hull above the main body of the boat that allowed the use of shorter periscopes. There is a propeller (or pump jet) at the rear and various hydrodynamic control fins as well as ballast tanks. Smaller, deep diving and specialty submarines may deviate significantly from this traditional layout.

MILITARY USAGE

The first use of a submarine in combat was the Action of 17 February 1864 during the American Civil War. The Confederate States Navy vessel CSS *Hunley* became the first submarine to sink an enemy vessel in combat, the USS *Housatonic*.

Before and during World War II, the primary role of the submarine was anti-surface ship warfare. Submarines would attack either on the surface or submerged, using torpedoes or (on the surface) deck guns. They were particularly effective in sinking Allied transatlantic shipping in both World Wars, and in disrupting Japanese supply routes and naval operations in the Pacific in World War II.

Mine-laying submarines were developed in the early part of the 20th century. The facility was used in both World Wars. Submarines were also used for inserting and removing covert agents and military forces, for intelligence-gathering and to rescue aircrew during large-scale air attacks on islands, where the airmen would be told of safe places to crash-land damaged aircraft so the submarine crew could rescue them. Submarines could carry cargo through hostile waters or act as supply vessels for other submarines.

Submarines could usually locate and attack other submarines only on the surface, although HMS *Venturer* managed to sink *U-864* with a four torpedo spread while both were submerged. The British developed a specialized anti-submarine submarine in World War I, the R class. After World War II, with the development of the homing torpedo, better sonar systems, and nuclear propulsion, submarines also became able to hunt each other effectively.

The development of submarine-launched nuclear missiles and submarine-launched cruise missiles gave submarines a substantial and long-ranged ability to attack both land and sea targets with a variety of weapons ranging from cluster bombs to nuclear weapons.

The primary defence of a submarine lies in its ability to remain concealed in the depths of the ocean. Early submarines could be detected underwater by the sound they made. Water is an excellent conductor of sound, and submarines can detect and track comparatively noisy surface ships from long distances. Modern submarines are built with an emphasis on stealth. Advanced propeller designs, extensive sound-reducing insulation, and special machinery allow a submarine to be as quiet as ambient ocean noise, making them extremely difficult to detect. It takes specialized technology to find and attack modern submarines.

Active sonar uses the reflection of a sound emitted from the search equipment to detect submarines. It has been used since World War II by surface ships, submarines or even aircraft, but it gives away the position of the emitter and is susceptible to counter-measures.

A concealed military submarine is a real threat and, because of its stealth, it can force an enemy navy to waste resources searching large areas of ocean and protecting all ships against possible attack. This advantage was vividly demonstrated in the 1982 Falklands War when the British SSN HMS *Conqueror* sank the Argentine cruiser *General Belgrano*. After the sinking the

Argentine Navy recognised that they had no effective defence against submarine attack, and the Argentine surface fleet withdrew to port for the remainder of the war, though an Argentine submarine remained at sea.

Civil Uses

Although the majority of the world's submarines are military ones, there are some civil submarines. They have a variety of uses, including tourism, exploration, oil and gas platform inspections and pipeline surveys. The first tourist submarine was launched in 1985, and by 1997 there were 45 of them operating around the world. A semi-civilian use was the adaption of U-boats for cargo transport during World War I and World War II.

TECHNOLOGY

Submersion and Trimming

All surface ships, as well as surfaced submarines, are in a positively buoyant condition, weighing less than the volume of water they would displace if fully submerged. To submerge hydrostatically, a ship must have negative buoyancy, either by increasing its own weight or decreasing its displacement of water. To control their weight, submarines have ballast tanks, which can be filled with outside water or pressurized air.

For general submersion or surfacing, submarines use the forward and aft tanks, called Main Ballast Tanks or MBTs, which are filled with water to submerge, or filled with air to surface. Under submerged conditions, MBTs generally remain flooded, which simplifies their design, and on many submarines these tanks are a section of interhull space. For more precise and quick control of depth, submarines use smaller Depth Control Tanks or DCTs, also called hard tanks due to their ability to withstand higher pressure. The amount of water in depth control tanks can be controlled either to reflect changes in outside conditions or change depth. Depth control tanks can be located either near the submarine's center of gravity, or separated along the submarine body to prevent affecting trim.

When submerged, the water pressure on submarine's hull can reach 4 MPa (580 psi) for steel submarines and up to 10 MPa

(1,500 psi) for titanium submarines like Komsomolets, while interior pressure remains relatively unchanged. This difference results in hull compression, which decreases displacement. Water density also increases with depth, as the salinity and pressure are higher, but this incompletely compensates for hull compression, so buoyancy decreases as depth increases. A submerged submarine is in an unstable equilibrium, having a tendency to either fall or float to the surface. Keeping a constant depth requires continual operation of either the depth control tanks or control surfaces.

Submarines in a neutral buoyancy condition are not intrinsically trim-stable. To maintain desired trim, submarines use forward and aft trim tanks. Pumps can move water between these, changing weight distribution, creating a moment pointing the sub up or down. A similar system is sometimes used to maintain stability. Sail of the French nuclear submarine *Casabianca;* note the diving planes, camouflaged masts, periscope, electronic warfare masts, door and windows.

The hydrostatic effect of variable ballast tanks is not the only way to control the submarine underwater. Hydrodynamic maneuvering is done by several surfaces, which can be moved to create hydrodynamic forces when a submarine moves at sufficient speed. The stern planes, located near the propeller and normally horizontal, serve the same purpose as the trim tanks, controlling the trim, and are commonly used, while other control surfaces may not be present on many submarines. The fairwater planes on the sail and/or bow planes on the main body, both also horizontal, are closer to the centre of gravity, and are used to control depth with less effect on the trim

When a submarine performs an emergency surfacing, all depth and trim methods are used simultaneously, together with propelling the boat upwards. Such surfacing is very quick, so the sub may even partially jump out of the water, potentially damaging submarine systems.

SUBMARINE HULL

Modern submarines are cigar-shaped. This design, visible in early submarines is sometimes called a "teardrop hull". It reduces the hydrodynamic drag when submerged, but decreases the seakeeping capabilities and increases drag while surfaced. Since the limitations of the propulsion systems of early submarines forced them to operate surfaced most of the time, their hull designs were a compromise. Because of the slow submerged speeds of those subs, usually well below 10 kt (18 km/h), the increased drag for underwater travel was acceptable. Late in World War II, when technology allowed faster and longer submerged operation and increased aircraft surveillance forced submarines to stay submerged, hull designs became teardrop shaped again to reduce drag and noise. On modern military submarines the outer hull is covered with a layer of sound-absorbing rubber, or anechoic plating, to reduce detection.

The occupied pressure hulls of deep diving submarines such as DSV *Alvin* are spherical instead of cylindrical. This allows a more even distribution of stress at the great depth. A titanium frame is usually affixed to the pressure hull, providing attachment for ballast and trim systems, scientific instrumentation, battery packs, syntactic flotation foam, and lighting.

A raised tower on top of a submarine accommodates the periscope and electronics masts, which can include radio, radar, electronic warfare, and other systems including the snorkel mast. In many early classes of submarines, the control room, or "conn", was located inside this tower, which was known as the "conning tower". Since then, the conn has been located within the hull of the submarine, and the tower is now called the "sail". The conn is distinct from the "bridge", a small open platform in the top of the sail, used for observation during surface operation.

"Bathtubs" are related to conning towers but are used on smaller submarines. The bathtub is a metal cylinder surrounding the hatch that prevents waves from breaking directly into the cabin. It is needed because surfaced submarines have limited freeboard, that is, they lie low in the water. Bathtubs help prevent swamping the vessel.

Single/double Hull

Modern submarines and submersibles, as well as the oldest ones, usually have a single hull. Large submarines generally have an additional hull or hull sections outside. This external hull, which actually forms the shape of submarine, is called the outer hull (*casing* in the Royal Navy) or light hull, as it does not have to withstand a pressure difference. Inside the outer hull there is a strong hull, or pressure hull, which withstands sea pressure and has normal atmospheric pressure inside.

As early as World War I, it was realized that the optimal shape for withstanding pressure conflicted with the optimal shape for seakeeping and minimal drag, and construction difficulties further complicated the problem. This was solved either by a compromise shape, or by using two hulls; internal for holding pressure, and external for optimal shape. Until the end of World War II, most submarines had an additional partial cover on the top, bow and stern, built of thinner metal, which was flooded when submerged. Germany went further with the Type XXI, the general predecessor of modern submarines, in which the pressure hull was fully enclosed inside the light hull, but optimized for submerged navigation, unlike earlier designs that were optimized for surface operation.

After World War II, approaches split. The Soviet Union changed its designs, basing them on German developments. All post-World War II heavy Soviet and Russian submarines are built with a double hull structure. American and most other Western submarines switched to a primarily single-hull approach. They still have light hull sections in the bow and stern, which house main ballast tanks and provide a hydrodynamically optimized shape, but the main cylindrical hull section has only a single plating layer. The double hulls are being considered for future submarines in the United States to improve payload capacity, stealth and range

Pressure Hull

The pressure hull is generally constructed of thick high strength steel with a complex structure and high strength reserve, and is separated with watertight bulkheads into several compartments. There are also examples of more than two hulls in a submarine, like the Typhoon class, which has two main pressure hulls and three smaller ones for control room, torpedoes and steering gear, with the missile launch system between the main hulls. The dive depth cannot be increased easily. Simply making the hull thicker increases the weight and requires reduction of onboard equipment weight, ultimately resulting in a *bathyscaphe*. This is acceptable for civilian research submersibles, but not military submarines.

World War I submarines had hulls of carbon steel, with a 100-metre (330 ft) maximum depth. During World War II, high-strength alloyed steel was introduced, allowing 200-metre (660 ft) depths. High-strength alloy steel remains the primary material for submarines today, with 250–400-metre (820–1,300 ft) depths, which cannot be exceeded on a military submarine without design compromises. To exceed that limit, a few submarines were built with titanium hulls. Titanium can be stronger than steel, lighter, and is not ferromagnetic, important for stealth. Titanium submarines were built by the Soviet Union, which developed specialized high-strength alloys. It has produced several types of titanium submarines. Titanium alloys allow a major increase in depth, but other systems need to be redesigned to cope, so test depth was limited to 1,000 metres (3,300 ft) for the Soviet submarine *Komsomolets*, the deepest-diving combat submarine. An Alfa-class submarine may have successfully operated at 1,300 metres (4,300 ft), though continuous operation at such depths would produce excessive stress on many submarine systems. Titanium does not flex as readily as steel, and may become brittle during many dive cycles. Despite its benefits, the high cost of titanium construction led to the abandonment of titanium submarine construction as the Cold War ended. Deep diving civilian submarines have used thick acrylic pressure hulls.

The deepest deep diving submarine to date is *Trieste* departed San Diego on October 5, 1959 for Guam aboard the freighter *Santa Maria* to participate in *Project Nekton*, a series of very deep dives in the Mariana Trench. On January 23, 1960, *Trieste* reached the ocean floor in the Challenger Deep (the deepest southern part of the Mariana Trench), carrying Jacques Piccard (son of Auguste) and Lieutenant Don Walsh, USN. This was the first time a vessel, manned or unmanned, had reached the deepest point in the Earth's oceans. The onboard systems indicated a depth of 11,521 metres (37,799 ft), although this was later revised to 10,916 metres (35,814 ft) and more accurate measurements made in 1995 have found the Challenger Deep to be slightly shallower, at 10,911 metres (35,797 ft).

The task of building a pressure hull is very difficult, as it must withstand pressures up to that of its required diving depth. When the hull is perfectly round in cross-section, the pressure is evenly distributed, and causes only hull compression. If the shape is not perfect, the hull is bent, with several points heavily strained. Inevitable minor deviations are resisted by stiffener rings, but even a one inch (25 mm) deviation from roundness results in over 30 percent decrease of maximal hydrostatic load and consequently dive depth. The hull must therefore be constructed with high precision. All hull parts must be welded without defects, and all joints are checked multiple times with different methods, contributing to the high cost of modern submarines. (For example, each *Virginia*-class attack submarine costs US$2.6 billion, over US$200,000 per ton of displacement.)

Propulsion

Originally, submarines were human propelled. The first mechanically driven submarine was the 1863 French *Plongeur,* which used compressed air for propulsion. Anaerobic propulsion was first employed by the Spanish *Ictineo II* in 1864, which used a solution of zinc, manganese dioxide, and potassium chlorate to generate sufficient heat to power a steam engine, while also providing oxygen for the crew. A similar system was not employed again until 1940 when the German Navy tested a hydrogen peroxide-based system, the Walter turbine, on the experimental V-80 submarine and later on the naval *U-791* and type XVII submarines.

Until the advent of nuclear marine propulsion, most 20th century submarines used batteries for running underwater and gasoline (petrol) or diesel engines on the surface, and for battery recharging. Early submarines used gasoline, but this quickly gave way to kerosene (paraffin), then diesel, because of reduced flammability. Diesel-electric became the standard means of propulsion. The diesel or gasoline engine and the electric motor, separated by clutches, were initially on the same shaft driving the propeller. This allowed the engine to drive the electric motor as a generator to recharge the batteries and also propel the submarine. The clutch between the motor and the engine would be disengaged when the submarine dove, so that the motor could drive the propeller. The motor could have multiple armatures on the shaft, which could be electrically coupled in series for slow speed and in parallel for high speed. (These connections were called "group down" and "group up", respectively.)

Electric transmission

Early submarines used a direct mechanical connection between the engine and propeller, switching between diesel engines for surface running, and electric motors for submerged propulsion. In 1928 the United States Navy's Bureau of Engineering proposed a diesel-electric transmission; instead of driving the propeller directly while running on the surface, the submarine's diesel would drive a generator which could either charge the submarine's batteries or drive the electric motor. This meant that motor speed was independent of the diesel engine's speed, and the diesel could run at an optimum and non-critical speed, while one or more of the diesel engines could be shut down for maintenance while the submarine continued to run using battery power. The concept was pioneered in 1929 in the S-class submarines *S-3*, *S-6*, and *S-7* to test the concept. No other navy adopted the system before 1945, apart from the Royal Navy's U-class submarines, though some submarines of the Imperial Japanese Navy used separate diesel generators for low speed running.

Other advantages of such an arrangement were that a submarine could travel slowly with the engines at full power to recharge the batteries quickly, reducing time on the surface or on snorkel. It was then possible to insulate the noisy diesel engines from the pressure hull, making the submarine quieter. Additionally, diesel-electric transmissions were more compact.

Air-independent Propulsion

During the Second World War, German Type XXI submarines were designed to carry hydrogen peroxide for long-term, fast air-independent propulsion, but were ultimately built with very large batteries instead. At the end of the War, the British and Russians experimented with hydrogen peroxide/kerosene (paraffin) engines which could be used surfaced and submerged. The results were not encouraging; although the Russians deployed a class of submarines with this engine type (codenamed Quebec by NATO), they were considered unsuccessful. Today several navies use air-independent propulsion. Notably Sweden uses Stirling technology on the *Gotland*-class and *Södermanland*-class submarines. The Stirling engine is heated by burning diesel fuel with liquid oxygen from cryogenic tanks. A newer development in air-independent propulsion is hydrogen fuel cells, first used on the German Type 212 submarine, with nine 34 kW or two 120 kW cells and soon to be used in the new Spanish S-80 class submarines

Nuclear Power

Steam power was resurrected in the 1950s with a nuclear-powered steam turbine driving a generator. By eliminating the need for atmospheric oxygen, the length of time that a modern submarine could remain submerged was limited only by its food stores, as breathing air was recycled and fresh water distilled from seawater. Nuclear-powered submarines have a relatively small battery and diesel engine/generator powerplant for emergency use if the reactors must be shut down.

Nuclear power is now used in all large submarines, but due to the high cost and large size of nuclear reactors, smaller submarines still use diesel-electric propulsion. The ratio of larger to smaller submarines depends on strategic needs. The US Navy, French Navy, and the Royal Navy operate only nuclear submarines, which is explained by the need for distant operations. Other major operators rely on a mix of nuclear submarines for strategic purposes and diesel-electric submarines for defence. Most fleets have no nuclear submarines, due to the limited availability of nuclear power and submarine technology.

Diesel-electric submarines have a stealth advantage over their nuclear counterparts. Nuclear submarines generate noise from coolant pumps and turbo-machinery needed to operate the reactor, even at low power levels. Some nuclear submarines such as the American *Ohio* class do not have coolant pumps, etc. in the reactors, and are quieter than electric subs. A conventional submarine operating on batteries is almost completely silent, the only noise coming from the shaft bearings, propeller, and flow noise around the hull, all of which stops when the sub hovers in mid water to listen. Commercial submarines usually rely only on batteries, since they never operate independently of a mother ship.

ALTERNATIVE PROPULSION

COMMUNICATION

95, Solveig Krey of the Royal Norwegian Navy became the first female officer to assume command on a military submarine, HNoMS *Kobben*.The British Royal Navy also does not permit women to serve on its submarines because of "medical concerns for the safety of the foetus and hence its mother" due to the potentially compromised air quality onboard submarines. It was similarly dangers to the pregnant woman and her fetus that barred females from submarine service in Sweden 1983, when all other positions where made available for them in the Swedish Navy. Pregnant woman are still not allowed to serve on submarines in Sweden. However, the policy makers thought that it was discriminatory with a general ban and demanded that females should be tried on their individual merits and have their suitability evaluated and compared to other candidates. Further, the risk that a female submariner should be unaware of getting pregnant was deemed to be very low.

Women have served on U.S. Navy surface ships since 1993 but do not serve on submarines. The Navy only allows three exceptions for women being on board military submarines: female civilian technicians for a few days at most; women midshipmen on an overnight during summer training for both Navy ROTC and Naval Academy; family members for one-day dependent cruises.

Both the U.S. and British navies operate nuclear-powered submarines which deploy for periods of six months or longer, whereas other navies which permit women on submarines operate conventionally powered submarines, which deploy for much shorter periods, usually only for one or two months. No nation using nuclear submarines currently permits women to serve onboard them. Removing the ban in the U.S. Navy has been put to congressional lawmakers by Joint Chiefs Chairman Adm.

Michael Mullen, following a review by Navy Secretary Ray Mabus and Chief of Naval Operations Adm. Gary Roughead.

Life Support Systems

With nuclear power, submarines can remain submerged for months at a time. Diesel submarines must periodically resurface or snorkel to recharge their batteries. Most modern military submarines generate breathing oxygen by electrolysis of water. Atmosphere control equipment includes a CO_2 scrubber, which uses an amine absorbent to remove the gas from air and diffuse it into waste pumped overboard. A machine that uses a catalyst to convert carbon monoxide into carbon dioxide (removed by the CO_2 scrubber) and bonds hydrogen produced from the ship's storage battery with oxygen in the atmosphere to produce water, is also used. An atmosphere monitoring system samples the air from different areas of the ship for nitrogen, oxygen, hydrogen, R-12 and R-114 refrigerants, carbon dioxide, carbon monoxide, and other gases. Poisonous gases are removed, and oxygen is replenished by use of an oxygen bank located in a main ballast tank. Some heavier submarines have two oxygen bleed stations (forward and aft). The oxygen in the air is sometimes kept a few percent less than atmospheric concentration to reduce fire danger.

Fresh water is produced by either an evaporator or a reverse osmosis unit. The primary use for fresh water is to provide feed water for the reactor and steam propulsion plants. It is also available for showers, sinks, cooking and cleaning once propulsion plant needs have been met. Seawater is used to flush toilets, and the resulting "black water" is stored in a sanitary tank until it is blown overboard using pressurized air or pumped overboard by using a special sanitary pump. The method for blowing sanitaries overboard is difficult to operate, and the German Type VIIC boat *U-1206* was lost with casualties because of a mistake with the toilet Water from showers and sinks is stored separately in "grey water" tanks, which are pumped overboard using the drain pump.

Trash on modern large submarines is usually disposed of using a tube called a Trash Disposal Unit (TDU), where it is compacted into a galvanized steel can. At the bottom of the TDU is a large ball valve. An ice plug is set on top of the ball valve to protect it, the cans atop the ice plug. The top breech door is shut, and the TDU is flooded and equalized with sea pressure, the ball valve is opened and the cans fall out assisted by scrap iron weights in the cans. The TDU is also flushed with seawater to ensure it is completely empty and the ball valve is clear before shutting the valve.

HISTORY OF SUBMARINES

The first submersible with reliable information on its construction was built in 1620 by Cornelius Jacobszoon Drebbel, a Dutchman in the service of James I of England. It was created to the standards of the design outlined by English mathematician William Bourne. It was propelled by means of oars. The precise nature of the submarine type is a matter of some controversy; some claim that it was merely a bell towed by a boat. Two improved types were tested in the Thames between 1620 and 1624. In 2002 a two-person version of Bourne's design was built for the BBC TV programme *Building the Impossible* by Mark Edwards, and successfully rowed under water at Dorney Lake, Eton.

Though the first submersible vehicles were tools for exploring under water, it did not take long for inventors to recognize their military potential. The strategic advantages of submarines were set out by Bishop John Wilkins of Chester, England, in *Mathematicall Magick* in 1648:

1. Tis private: a man may thus go to any coast in the world invisibly, without discovery or prevented in his journey.
2. Tis safe, from the uncertainty of Tides, and the violence of Tempests, which do never move the sea above five or six paces deep. From Pirates and Robbers which do so infest other voyages; from ice and great frost, which do so much endanger the passages towards the Poles.
3. It may be of great advantages against a Navy of enemies, who by this may be undermined in the water and blown up.
4. It may be of special use for the relief of any place besieged by water, to convey unto them invisible supplies; and so likewise for the surprisal of any place that is accessible by water.

5. It may be of unspeakable benefit for submarine experiments.

The First Military Submarines

The first military submarine was *Turtle* (1775), a hand-powered egg-shaped device designed by the American David Bushnell to accommodate a single person. It was the first verified submarine capable of independent underwater operation and movement, and the first to use screws for propulsion. During the American Revolutionary War, *Turtle* (operated by Sgt. Ezra Lee, Continental Army) tried and failed to sink the British warship HMS *Eagle*, flagship of the blockaders in New York harbor on September 7, 1776.

In 1800, France built a human-powered submarine designed by American Robert Fulton, the *Nautilus*. The French eventually gave up on the experiment in 1804, as did the British when they later considered Fulton's submarine design. During the War of 1812, in 1814, Silas Halsey lost his life while using a submarine in an unsuccessful attack on a British warship stationed in New London harbor. In 1851, a Bavarian artillery corporal, Wilhelm Bauer, took a submarine designed by him called the *Brandtaucher* (incendiary-diver) to sea in Kiel Harbour. This submarine was built by August Howaldt and powered by a treadwheel. It sank but the three crew managed to escape. The submarine was raised in 1887 and is on display in a museum in Dresden.

SUBMARINES IN THE AMERICAN CIVIL WAR

During the American Civil War, the Union was the first to field a submarine. The French-designed *Alligator* was the first U.S. Navy sub and the first to feature compressed air (for air supply) and an air filtration system. Initially hand-powered by oars, it was converted after 6 months to a screw propeller powered by a hand crank. With a crew of 20, it was larger than Confederate submarines. *Alligator* was 47 feet (14.3 m) long and about 4 feet (1.2 m) in diameter. It was lost in a storm off Cape Hatteras on April 1, 1863 with no crew and under tow to its first combat deployment at Charleston.

The Confederate States of America fielded several human-powered submarines. The first Confederate submarine was the 30-foot (9 m) long *Pioneer* which sank a target schooner using a towed mine during tests on Lake Pontchartrain, but was not used in combat. It was scuttled after New Orleans was captured and in 1868 was sold for scrap. The Bayou St. John Confederate Submarine was also scuttled without seeing combat, and is now on display at the Louisiana State Museum.

The Confederate submarine *H. L. Hunley* (named for one of its financiers, Horace Lawson Hunley) was intended for attacking the North's ships, which were blockading the South's seaports. The submarine had a long pole with an explosive charge in the bow, called a spar torpedo. The sub had to approach an enemy vessel, attach an explosive, move away, and then detonate it. The sub was extremely hazardous to operate, and had no air supply other than what was contained inside the main compartment. On two occasions, the sub sank; on the first occasion half the crew died and on the second, the entire eight-man crew (including Hunley himself) drowned. On February 17, 1864 *Hunley* sank USS *Housatonic* off Charleston Harbor, the first time a submarine successfully sank another ship, though it sank in the same engagement shortly after signaling its success. Submarines did not have a major impact on the outcome of the war, but did portend their coming importance to naval warfare and increased interest in their use in naval warfare.

South America

The first submarine in South America was the *Hipopotamo*, tested in Ecuador on September 18, 1837. It was built by Jose Rodriguez Lavandera, who successfully crossed the Guayas River in Guayaquil accompanied by Jose Quevedo. Rodriguez Lavandera enrolled in the Navy in 1823, becoming a Lieutenant by 1830. The *Hipopotamo* crossed the Guayas on two more occasions, but it was then abandoned because of lack of funding and interest from the government. The submarine *Flach* was commissioned in 1865 by the Chilean government during the war of Chile and Peru against Spain (1864-1866). It was built by the German engineer Karl Flach. The submarine sank during tests in Valparaiso bay on May 3, 1866, with the entire eleven-man crew.

Mechanically-powered Submarines (late 19th Century)

The first submarine not relying on human power for propulsion was the French *Plongeur,* launched in 1863, and using compressed air at 180 psi (1241 kPa). The first combustion-powered submarine was *Ictineo II,* designed in Spain by Narcís Monturiol. Originally launched in 1864 as human-powered, propelled by 16 , it was converted to peroxide propulsion and steam in 1867. The 14 meter (46 ft) craft was designed for a crew of two, could dive to 30 metres (96 ft), and demonstrated dives of two hours. On the surface it ran on a steam engine, but underwater such an engine would quickly consume the submarine's oxygen; so Monturiol invented an air-independent propulsion system. While the air-independent power system drove the screw, the chemical process driving it also released oxygen into the hull for the crew and an auxiliary steam engine. Monturiol's fully functional, double hulled vessels also solved pressure and buoyancy control problems that had bedeviled earlier designs

In 1870, the French writer Jules Verne published the science fiction classic *20,000 Leagues under the Sea,* which concerns the adventures of a maverick inventor in *Nautilus,* a submarine more advanced than any at the time. The story inspired inventors to build more advanced submarines.

In 1879, the Peruvian government, during the War of the Pacific, commissioned and built the fully operational submarine *Toro Submarino.* It never saw military action before being scuttled after the defeat of that country in the war to prevent its capture by the enemy. The first submarine to be mass-produced was human-powered. It was the submarine of the Polish inventor Stefan Drzewiecki—50 units were built in 1881 for the Russian government. In 1884 the same inventor built an eléctric-powered submarine.

The Nordenfelt-designed Ottoman submarine *Abdülhamid* (1886) was the first submarine in the world to fire a torpedo while submerged. It and its sister ship, *Abdülmecid* (1887), were built in pieces by Des Vignes (Chertsey) and Vickers (Sheffield) in England, and were assembled at the Taþkýzak Naval Shipyard in Istanbul, Turkey.

Discussions between the English clergyman and inventor George Garrett and the industrially and commercially adept Swede Thorsten Nordenfelt led to a series of steam-powered submarines. The first was the *Nordenfelt I*, a 56 tonne, 19.5 metre (64 ft) vessel similar to Garret's ill-fated *Resurgam* (1879), with a range of 240 kilometres (150 mi, 130 nm), armed with a single torpedo, in 1885. Like *Resurgam*, *Nordenfelt I* operated on the surface by steam, then shut down its engine to dive. While submerged the submarine released pressure generated when the engine was running on the surface to provide propulsion for some distance underwater. Greece, fearful of the return of the Ottomans, purchased it. Nordenfelt then built *Nordenfelt II* (*Abdülhamid*) in 1886 and *Nordenfelt III* (*Abdülmecid*) in 1887, a pair of 30 metre (100 ft) submarines with twin torpedo tubes, for the Ottoman navy. *Abdülhamid* became the first submarine in history to fire a torpedo submerged Nordenfelt's efforts culminated in 1887 with *Nordenfelt IV* which had twin motors and twin torpedoes. It was sold to the Russians, but proved unstable, ran aground, nd was scrapped.

On September 8, 1888, an electrically powered vessel built by the Spanish engineer and sailor Isaac Peral for the Spanish Navy was launched. It had two torpedoes, new air systems, and a hull shape, propeller, and cruciform external controls anticipating much later designs. Its underwater speed was ten knots (19 km/h). In June 1890 Peral's submarine launched a torpedo while submerged. Its ability to fire torpedoes under water while maintaining full propulsive power and control has led some to call it the first U-boat. After many successful dives the project was scrapped because of the difficulties of recharging at sea and the short range of battery-powered vessels. Shortly after, the French *Gymnote* was launched on September 24, 1888. The electrically-powered *Gymnote*, another fully functional military submarine, completed 2,000 dives successfully. Many more designs were built at this time by various inventors, but submarines were not to become effective weapons until the 20th century.

Late 19th century to World War I

The turn of the 19th century marked a pivotal time in the development of submarines, with a number of important technologies making their debut, as well as the widespread adoption and fielding of submarines by a number of nations. Diesel electric propulsion would become the dominant power system and equipment such as the periscope would become standardized. Large numbers of experiments were done by countries on effective tactics and weapons for submarines, all of which would culminate in them making a large impact on the coming World War I.

In 1896, the Irish-American inventor John Philip Holland designed submarines that, for the first time, made use of internal combustion engine power on the surface and electric battery power for submerged operations. The *Holland VI* was launched on May 17, 1897 at Navy Lt. Lewis Nixon's Crescent Shipyard of Elizabeth, New Jersey. On April 11, 1900 the United States Navy purchased the revolutionary *Holland VI* and renamed it the USS *Holland* (SS-1), America's first commissioned submarine. (John P. Holland's company, the Holland Torpedo Boat Company/Electric Boat Company became General Dynamics "Cold War" progeny and is arguably the builder of the world's most technologically advanced submarines today).

A prototype version of the *Plunger*-class or A-class submarines, the *Fulton*, was developed at Nixon's Crescent Shipyard for the United States Navy before the construction of the A-class submarines there in 1901. A naval architect and shipbuilder from the United Kingdom, Arthur Leopold Busch, superintended the development of these first submarines for Holland's company. However the *Fulton* was never purchased by the U.S. Navy and was eventually sold to the Imperial Russian Navy during the Russo-Japanese War of 1904-1905. Two other A-class vessels were built on the West Coast of (USA) at Mare Island Naval Shipyard/ Union Iron Works circa 1901. In 1902, Holland received a patent for his persistent pursuit to perfect the underwater naval craft. By this time, Holland was no longer in control of the day-to-day operations at Electric Boat, as others were now at the helm of the company he once founded. The acumen of business were now in control of these operations as Holland was forced to step down. His resignation from the company was to be effective as of April 1904.

Many other countries became interested in Holland's products around this time. Holland's innovations and ideas were considered to be the most technologically advanced at the time and were universally acknowledged as such. From 1901 onwards some of Holland's vessels were purchased by the United States Navy and other governments including the United Kingdom, the Imperial Russian Navy, Imperial Japanese Navy and the Royal Netherlands Navy.

Commissioned in June 1900, the French steam and electric submarine *Narval* introduced the classic double-hull design, with a pressure hull inside the outer light hull. These 200-ton ships had a range of over 100 miles (160 km) on the surface, and over 10 miles (16 km) underwater. The French submarine *Aigrette* in 1904 further improved the concept by using a diesel rather than a gasoline engine for surface power. Large numbers of these submarines were built, with seventy-six completed before 1914.

Submarines during World War I

Military submarines first made a significant impact in World War I. Forces such as the U-boats of Germany saw action in the First Battle of the Atlantic, and were responsible for the sinking of *Lusitania*, which was sunk as a result of unrestricted submarine warfare and is often cited among the reasons for the entry of the United States into the war.

The U-boats' ability to function as practical war machines relied on new tactics, their numbers, and submarine technologies such as combination diesel-electric power system developed in the preceding years. More submersibles than true submarines, U-boats operated primarily on the surface using regular engines, submerging occasionally to attack under battery power. They were roughly triangular in cross-section, with a distinct keel to control rolling while surfaced, and a distinct bow.

Interwar Developments

Various new submarine designs were developed during the interwar years. Among the most notorious ones were submarine aircraft carriers, equipped with a waterproof hangar and steam catapult to launch and recover one or more small seaplanes. The submarine and its plane could then act as a reconnaissance unit ahead of the fleet, an essential role at a time when radar still did not exist. The first example was the British HMS *M2*, followed by the French *Surcouf*, and numerous aircraft-carrying submarines in the Imperial Japanese Navy.

Submarines during World War II

Germany had the largest submarine fleet during World War II. Due to the Treaty of Versailles limiting the surface navy, the rebuilding of the German surface forces had only begun in earnest a year before the outbreak of World War II. Expecting to be able to defeat the Royal Navy through underwater warfare, the German High Command pursued commerce raiding and immediately stopped all construction on capital surface ships save the nearly completed *Bismarck*-class battleships and two cruisers, switching its resources to submarines, which could be built more quickly. Though it took most of 1940 to expand the production facilities and get the mass production started, more than a thousand submarines were built by the end of the war.

Germany put submarines to devastating effect in the Second Battle of the Atlantic in World War II, attempting but ultimately failing to cut off Britain's supply routes by sinking more merchant ships than Britain could replace. The supply lines were vital to Britain for food and industry, as well as armaments from the US. Although the U-boats had been updated in the intervening years, the major innovation was improved communications, encrypted using the famous Enigma cipher machine. This allowed for mass-attack tactics or "wolf packs" (Rudeltaktik), but was also ultimately the U-boats' downfall.

After putting to sea, U-boats operated mostly on their own, trying to find convoys in areas assigned to them by the High Command. If a convoy was found, the submarine did not attack immediately, but shadowed the convoy to allow other submarines in the area to find the convoy. These were then grouped into a larger striking force to attack the convoy simultaneously, preferably at night while surfaced.

From September 1939 to the beginning of 1943, the *Ubootwaffe* ("U-boat force") scored unprecedented success with these tactics, but were too few to have any decisive success. By the spring of 1943, German U-boat construction was at full capacity, but this was more than nullified by increased numbers of convoy escorts and aircraft, as well as technical advances like radar and sonar. Huff-Duff and Ultra allowed the Allies to route convoys around wolf packs when they detected them from their radio transmissions. The results were devastating: from March to July of that year, over 130 U-boats were lost, 41 in May alone. Concurrent Allied losses dropped dramatically, from 750,000 tons in March to only 188,000 in July. Although the Second battle of the Atlantic would continue to the last day of the war, the U-boat arm was unable to stem the tide of personnel and supplies, paving the way for Operation Torch, Operation Husky, and ultimately, D-Day. Winston Churchill wrote that the U-boat "peril" was the only thing that ever gave him cause to doubt the Allies' eventual victory.

Japan

The Imperial Japanese Navy started their submarine service with five *Holland* Type VII submarines purchased from the Electric Boat Company in 1904. Japan had the most varied fleet of submarines of World War II; including *Kaiten* crewed torpedoes, midget submarines (*Ko-hyoteki* and *Kairyu*), medium-range submarines, purpose-built supply submarines and long-range fleet submarines. They also had submarines with the highest submerged speeds during World War II (*I-200*-class submarines) and submarines that could carry multiple aircraft (*I-400*-class submarine). They were also equipped with one of the most advanced torpedoes of the conflict, the oxygen-propelled Type 95.

Nevertheless, despite their technical prowess, Japan had chosen to utilize its submarines for fleet warfare, and consequently were relatively unsuccessful, as warships were fast, maneuverable and well-defended compared to merchant ships. In 1942, a Japanese submarine sank one aircraft carrier, damaged one battleship, and damaged one destroyer (which sank later) from one torpedo salvo; and during the Battle of Midway were able to deliver the coup de grace to another fleet aircraft carrier. With the lack of fuel oil and air supremacy, Imperial submarines were not able to sustain those kind of results afterwards. By the end of the war, submarines were instead often used to transport supplies to island garrisons.

United States

The United States Navy used its submarine force to attack both warships and merchant shipping; and destroyed more Japanese shipping than all other weapons combined. This feat was considerably aided by the Imperial Japanese Navy's failure to provide adequate escort forces for the nation's merchant fleet.

Whereas Japan had the finest submarine torpedoes of the war, the U.S. Navy had the worst: the Mark 14 torpedo that ran ten feet too deep, tipped with a Mk VI exploder that was based on an unimproved version of the Mark V contact exploder but with an additional magnetic exploder, neither of which was reliable. The faulty depth control mechanism of the Mark 14 was corrected in August 1942, but field trials for the exploders were not ordered until mid-1943, when tests in Hawaii and Australia confirmed the flaws. Fully operational Mark 14 torpedoes were not put into service until September 1943. The Mark 15 torpedo used by US surface combatants had the same Mk VI exploder and was not fixed until late 1943. One attempt to correct the problems resulted in a wakeless, electric torpedo being placed in submarine service, but USS *Tang* and *Tullibee* were lost to self-inflicted hits by these torpedoes.

During World War II, 314 submarines served in the United States Navy, of which nearly 260 were deployed to the Pacific. On December 7, 1941, 111 boats were in commission; 203 submarines from the *Gato*, *Balao*, and *Tench* classes were commissioned during the war. During the war, 52 US submarines were lost to all causes, with 48 lost directly to hostilities; 3,505 sailors were lost, the highest percentage killed in action of any US service arm in World War II. US submarines sank 1,560 enemy vessels, a total tonnage of 5.3 million tons, including 8 aircraft carriers and over 200 warships.

United Kingdom

The Royal Navy Submarine Service was primarily used to enforce the classic British blockade role. It therefore chiefly operated in inshore waters and tended to only surface by night. Its major operating areas were around Norway, the Mediterranean (against the Axis supply routes to North Africa), and in the Far East. RN submarines operating out of Trincomalee and Australia were a constant threat to Japanese shipping passing through the Malacca Straits. .

In the war British submarines sank 2 million tons of enemy shipping and 57 major warships, the latter including 35 submarines. Amongst these is the only instance ever of a submarine sinking another submarine while both were submerged. This occurred when HMS *Venturer* engaged the *U864*; the *Venturer* crew manually computed a successful firing solution against a three-dimensionally manoeveuring target using techniques which became the basis of modern torpedo computer targeting systems. Seventy-four British submarines were lost, half probably to naval mines.

The Snorkel

Diesel-electric submarines need air to run their diesel engines, and so carried very large batteries for submerged operation. The need to recharge the batteries from the diesel engines limited the endurance of the submarine while submerged and required it to surface regularly for extended periods, during which it was especially vulnerable to detection and attack. The snorkel, a pre-war Dutch invention, was used to allow German submarines to run their diesel engines whilst running just under the surface, drawing air through a tube from the surface.

The German Navy also experimented with engines that would use hydrogen peroxide to allow diesel fuel to be used while submerged, but technical difficulties were great. The Allies experimented with a variety of detection systems, including chemical sensors to "smell" the exhaust of submarines. Cold-war diesel-electric submarines, such as the *Oberon* class, used batteries to power their electric motors in order to run silently. They recharged the batteries using the diesel engines without ever surfacing.

MODERN MILITARY SUBMARINES

The first launch of a cruise missile (SSM-N-8 Regulus) from a submarine occurred in July 1953 from the deck of USS *Tunny*, a World War II fleet boat modified to carry this missile with a nuclear warhead. *Tunny* and her sister boat *Barbero* were the United States's first nuclear deterrent patrol submarines. They were joined in 1958 by two purpose built Regulus submarines, *Grayback, Growler*, and, later, by the nuclear powered *Halibut*.

In the 1950s, nuclear power partially replaced diesel-electric propulsion. Equipment was also developed to extract oxygen from sea water. These two innovations gave submarines the ability to remain submerged for weeks or months, and enabled previously impossible voyages such as USS *Nautilus'* crossing of the North pole beneath the Arctic ice cap in 1958 and the USS *Triton*'s submerged circumnavigation of the world in 1960 Most of the naval submarines built since that time in the United States and the Soviet Union/Russia have been powered by nuclear reactors. The limiting factors in submerged endurance for these vessels are food supply and crew morale in the space-limited submarine. In 1959–1960, the first ballistic missile submarines were put into service by both the United States (*George Washington* class) and the Soviet Union (Hotel class) as part of the Cold War nuclear deterrent strategy.

While the greater endurance and performance from nuclear reactors makes nuclear submarines better for long-distance missions or the protection of a carrier battle group, their reactor cooling pumps have traditionally made them noisier, and thus easier to detect, than conventional diesel-electric submarines. Diesel-electrics have continued to be produced by both nuclear and non-nuclear powers as they lack this limitation, except when required to run the diesel engine to recharge the ship's battery. Recent technological advances in sound damping, noise isolation, and cancellation have made nuclear subs quieter and substantially eroded this advantage. Though far less capable regarding speed and weapons payload, conventional submarines are also cheaper to build. The introduction of air-independent propulsion boats, conventional diesel-electric submarines with some kind of auxiliary air-independent electricity generator, have led to increased sales of such types of submarines.

During the Cold War, the United States and the Soviet Union maintained large submarine fleets that engaged in cat-and-mouse games. The Soviet Union suffered the loss of at least four submarines during this period: *K-129* was lost in 1968 (which the CIA attempted to retrieve from the ocean floor with the Howard Hughes-designed ship *Glomar Explorer*), *K-8* in 1970, *K-219* in 1986, and *Komsomolets* in 1989 (which held a depth record among military submarines—1000 m).

Many other Soviet subs, such as *K-19* (the first Soviet nuclear submarine, and the first Soviet sub to reach the North Pole) were badly damaged by fire or radiation leaks. The US lost two nuclear submarines during this time: USS *Thresher* due to equipment failure during a test dive while at its operational limit, and USS *Scorpion* due to unknown causes.

During the Indo-Pakistani War of 1971, the Pakistan Navy's *Hangor* sank the Indian frigate INS *Khukri*.

This was the first kill by a submarine since World War II, and the only one until the United Kingdom employed nuclear-powered submarines against Argentina in 1982 during the Falklands War. The Argentine cruiser *General Belgrano* was sunk by HMS *Conqueror* (the first sinking by a nuclear-powered submarine in war). The PNS *Ghazi*, a *Tench*-class submarine on loan to Pakistan from the US, was sunk in the Indo-Pakistani War. It was the first submarine casualty since World War II during war time.

More recently, Russia has had three high profile submarine accidents. The *Kursk* went down with all hands in 2000; the *K-159* sank while being towed to a scrapyard in 2003, with nine lives lost; and the *Nerpa* had an accident with the fire-extinguishing system resulting in twenty deaths in late 2008.

ANTI-SUBMARINE WARFARE

An anti-submarine warfare or weapon is any one of a range of devices that are intended to act against a submarine, and its crew, to destroy (sink) the vessel or to destroy or reduce its capability as a weapon of war. An anti-submarine weapon can be integrated with an anti-submarine warfare (ASW) system, such as the US Navy Tactical Data System (NTDS) that controls air, land and sea-based weapon system threat detection and target acquisition. However, in its simplest sense it is a projectile, missile or bomb that is optimized to destroy submarines.

History

Prior to about 1890, naval weapons were used only against surface shipping. With the rise of the military submarine after this time, countermeasures were considered for use against them. The first submarine installation of torpedo tubes was in 1885 and the first ship was sunk by a submarine launched torpedo in 1887. There were only two ways of countering the military submarine initially, ramming them or sinking them with gunfire. However once they were submerged they were largely immune until they had to surface again. By the start of the First World War there were nearly 300 submarines in service with another 80 in the pipeline.

World War I marked the first earnest conflict involving significant use of submarines and consequently marked the beginning of major efforts to counter that threat. In particular, the United Kingdom was desperate to defeat the German U-Boat threat against British merchant shipping. When the bombs that it employed were found to be ineffective it began equipping its destroyers with simple depth charges that could be dropped into the water around a suspected submarine's location. During this period it was found that explosions of these charges were more efficient if the charges were set to explode below or above the submarine. However many other techniques were used, including minefields, barrages and Q-ships and the use of cryptanalysis against intercepted radio messages. The airship ("blimp") was used to drop bombs but fixed wing aircraft were mostly used for reconnaissance. However the most effective countermeasure was the convoy. In 1918 U-boat losses became unbearably high. During the war a total of 178 U-boats were sunk : British submarines operated in the Baltic, North Sea and Atlantic as well as the Mediterranean and Black Sea. Most of the losses were due to mines but two were torpedoed. French, Italian and Russian submarines were also destroyed.

Before the war ended, the need for forward-throwing weapons had been recognized by the British and trials began. Hydrophones had been developed and were becoming effective as detection and location devices. Also, aircraft and airships had flown with depth bombs (aerial depth charges), albeit quite small ones with poor explosives. In addition, the specialist hunter-killer submarine had appeared, HMS *R-1*.

Inter-war

The main developments in this period were in detection, with both active sonar (ASDIC) and radar becoming effective. The British integrated the sonar with fire control and weapons to form an integrated system for warships. Germany was banned from having a submarine fleet but began construction in secret during the 1930s. When war broke out it had 21 submarines at sea. In the inter-war period Britain and France had experimented with several novel types of submarine. New sonars and weapons were developed for them.

Atlantic/Mediterranean Theatre

By the time of World War II, anti-submarine weapons had been developed somewhat, but during that war, there was a renewal of all-out submarine warfare by Germany as well as widespread use of submarines by most of the other combatants. The effective use of depth charges required the combined resources and skills of many individuals during an attack. Sonar information, helmsmen, depth charge crews and the movement of other ships had to be carefully coordinated in order to deliver a successful depth charge attack. As the Battle of the Atlantic wore on, British and Commonwealth forces in particular proved particularly adept at depth charge tactics, and formed some of the first destroyer hunter-killer groups to actively seek out and destroy German U-boats.

Mk. 17 depth bomb is being unloaded from a SOC Seagull scout plane on board the USS Philadelphia (CL-41) during an Atlantic U-boat sweep near Panama in June 1942. Air-dropped depth bombs were normally set to explode at a shallow depth, while the submarine was crash-diving to escape attack. Aircraft were very successful in not only attacking U-boats, but also in disrupting U-boats from carrying out attacks against ships. Some were fitted with a searchlight as well as bombs.

A host of new anti-submarine weapons were developed. Forward-throwing anti-submarine mortars were introduced in

1942 to prevent loss of sonar contact. These mortars used small depth charges, the first being codenamed *Hedgehog*. One type of charge created entire patterns of explosions underwater around a potential enemy, while the second type was of round was fitted with contact detonators, meaning the warhead exploded only upon contact with the submarine. A later design enabled a pursuing destroyer or destroyer escort to maintain continual sonar contact until a definite 'hit' was achieved. Additionally, new weapons were designed for use by aircraft, rapidly increasing their importance in fighting submarines. The development of the FIDO (Mk 24 mine) anti-submarine homing torpedo in 1943 (which could be dropped from aircraft) was a significant contributor to the rising number of German sub sinkings.

Hedgehog, a 24 barreled anti-submarine mortar, mounted on the forecastle of the destroyer HMS *Westcott*, 28 November 1945. The 27-year veteran *Westcott* claimed the first-ever kill by Hedgehog February 2, 1942, when she sank *U-581*.

Pacific Theatre

Japan, the United States, Great Britain, The Netherlands, and Australia all employed anti-submarine forces in the Pacific Theatre during World War II. Because the Japanese Navy tended to utilize its submarines against capital ships such as cruisers, battleships and aircraft carriers, U.S. and Allied anti-submarine efforts concentrated their work in support of fleet defence.

Early Japanese submarines were not very maneuverable under water, could not dive very deep, and lacked radar. Later in the war, Japanese submarines were fitted with radar scanning equipment for improved hunting while surfaced. However, these radar-equipped submarines were in some instances sunk due to the ability of U.S. radar receivers to detect their tell-tale scanning emissions. For example, *Batfish* sank three Japanese radar-equipped submarines in the span of four days. In 1944, U.S. anti-submarine forces began to employ the FIDO (Mk 24 mine) air-dropped homing torpedo against submerged Japanese subs with considerable success.

In contrast, Allied submarines were largely committed against Japanese merchant shipping. As a consequence, Japanese anti-submarine forces were forced to spread their efforts to defend the entirety of their merchant shipping lanes, not only to resupply their forces, but also to continue the necessary importation of war material to the Japanese home islands.

At first, Japanese anti-submarine defenses proved less than effective against U.S. submarines. Japanese sub detection gear was not as advanced as that of some other nations.

The primary Japanese anti-submarine weapon for most of WWII was the depth charge, and Japanese depth charge attacks by its surface forces initially proved fairly unsuccessful against U.S. fleet submarines. Unless caught in shallow water, a U.S. submarine commander could normally dive to a deeper depth in order to escape destruction, sometimes using temperature gradient barriers to escape pursuit. Additionally, during the first part of the war, the Japanese tended to set their depth charges too shallow, unaware that U.S. submarines possessed the ability to dive beyond 150 feet.

Unfortunately, the deficiencies of Japanese depth-charge tactics were revealed in a June 1943 press conference held by U.S. Congressman Andrew J. May, a member of the House Military Affairs Committee who had visited the Pacific theatre and received many confidential intelligence and operational briefings.

At the press conference, May revealed that American submarines had a high survivability because Japanese depth charges were fused to explode at too shallow a depth, typically 100 feet (because Japanese forces believed U.S. subs did not normally exceed this depth). Various press associations sent this story over their wires, and many newspapers, including one in Honolulu, thoughtlessly published it. Soon enemy depth charges were rearmed to explode at a more effective depth of 250 feet. Vice Admiral Charles A. Lockwood, commander of the U.S. submarine fleet in the Pacific, later estimated that May's revelation cost the navy as many as ten submarines and 800 crewmen.

In addition to resetting their depth charges to deeper depths, Japanese anti-submarine forces also began employing autogyro aircraft and Magnetic Anomaly Detection (MAD) equipment to sink U.S. subs, particularly those plying major shipping channels or operating near the home islands. Despite this onslaught, U.S.

sub sinkings of Japanese shipping continued to increase at a furious rate as more U.S. subs deployed each month to the Pacific. By the end of the war, U.S. submarines had destroyed more Japanese shipping than all other weapons combined, including aircraft.

POST-WAR DEVELOPMENTS

The four principal methods of delivering an acoustic homing torpedo or a Nuclear Depth Bomb at long range from a surface escort. Only the rocket-thrown weapons (*ASROC* and *Ikara*) are available for use in all-weather conditions and at instant readiness. The Cold War brought a new kind of conflict to submarine warfare. This war of development had both the United States and Soviet Union racing to develop better, stealthier and more potent submarines while consequently developing better and more accurate anti-submarine weapons and new delivery platforms, including the helicopter.

Attack submarines (SSKs and SSNs) were developed to include faster, longer range and more discriminating torpedoes. This, coupled with improvements to sonar systems, made ballistic missile submarines more vulnerable to attack submarines and also increased the Anti-Surface Warfare (ASuW) capabilities of attack subs.

SSBNs themselves as well as cruise-missile submarines (SSGNs) were fitted with increasingly more accurate and longer range missiles and received the greatest noise reduction technology. To counter this increasing threat torpedoes were honed to target submarines more effectively and new anti-submarine missiles and rockets were developed to give ships a longer-range anti-submarine capability. Ships, submarines and Maritime Patrol Aircraft (MPA) also received increasingly effective technology for locating submarines, e.g. Magnetic Anomaly Detectors (MAD) and improved sonar.

ANTI-SUBMARINE TECHNOLOGY

Many concepts have been tried to come up with ways of attacking submarines. The first component of an Anti-submarine attack is detection: anti-sub weapons cannot be successfully employed without first locating the enemy submarine.

Detection Equipment

Optical Detection

The "Mark I Eyeball" was the first submarine detection method, and remains an important method of target confirmation. This may now be supplemented by thermal techniques. However, the low "indiscretion rate" of modern submarines means that optical detection is now less successful.

Radio Intercept

The use of the "wolf pack" by submarines in both the first and second World Wars allowed interception of radio signals. Though these were encrypted, they were broken by the British at "Room 40" in the First World War and by Bletchley Park during the second. This allowed convoys to be diverted and hunter-killer groups to be targeted on the pack. Submarines now transmit using methods that are less susceptible to intercept.

Radar

Radar was a prime tool in World War II for locating surfaced submarines. After development of the snorkel, and then of nuclear-powered submarines, submarines rarely surfaced outside their home port, rendering direct radar detection largely useless. However, it is possible that radar can detect the surface effects produced by a submarine.

Sonar

Since World War II, sonar has emerged as the primary method of underwater detection of submarines. The most effective type has varied between active and passive, depending on the countermeasures taken by the submarine. Its versatility has increased with the development of air-dropped sonobuoys, which relay sonar signals to overhead aircraft, dipping sonar from helicopters and fixed long range systems.

Magnetic Anomaly Detection

A Magnetic Anomaly Detector (MAD) is an electronic magnetometer designed to measure magnetic field variations caused by large metal objects, such as the steel hull of a submarine.

Before the development of sonar buoys, MAD gear was often installed in aircraft to pick up shallow-submerged submarines. It is still used today.

Other non-acoustic methods

Submarine detector loops were one of the first ways of finding the presence of an underwater submarine. The "sniffer" for detecting diesel exhausts was developed in the Second World War. More recently indirect methods of submarine detection have been tried, mainly via its wake.

Anti-submarine Weapons

Anti-submarine weapons can be divided into three categories according to their mode of operation: Guided weapons, Non-guided weapons and Rocket-and Mortar weapons.

Guided anti-submarine weapons, such as torpedoes, seek out the submarine, either via its own sensors or from the launching platform's sensors. The advantage with this type of weapon is that it requires a relatively small payload since it detonates in direct contact or within a very close proximity of the submarine. The disadvantage is that this type of weapon can be decoyed and is adversely affected by stealth features of the submarine.

Non-guided anti-submarine weapons, such as mines and depth charges, are "dumb" weapons that has to be carried to the submarine or that the submarine has to come in close priximity of. This is to some degree compensated by a heavy payload, in some mines exceeding half a metric ton, but since the effect of an underwater explosion decreases with a factor of the the distance cubed, an increase in payload of a depth charge from 100 to 200 kg would not results in more than a few meters in killing radius.

Rocket-and mortar weapons, such as anti-submarine grenades and anti-submarine rockets, main advantage is the rapid response time since they are carried through the air to the target. Once dropped on top of the target, they also have the advantage of not being sensitive to decoys or stealth features. A hybrid of this category is the rocket lauched torpedo, which is carried to the proximity of the target via a rocket and therefore reduces the response time and gives the submarine less time to undertake coutermeasures or evasive manouvers. Finally, a submarine can of course also be destroyed by means of artillery fire and missiles in the rare case that a modern submarine surfaces, but these weapons are not specifically designed for submarines and their importance in modern anti-submarine warfare is very limited.

GUNS/MISSILES

Gunfire has been used to disable submarines from the First World War onwards, while a helicopter missile attack was used to disable the "Santa Fé" in the Falklands War.

Depth charge

The simplest of the anti-submarine weapons, the depth charge is a large canister filled with explosives and set to explode at a predetermined depth. The concussive effects of the explosion could damage a submarine from a distance, though a depth charge explosion had to be very close to break the submarine's hull. Air-dropped depth charges were referred to as 'depth bombs'; these were sometimes fitted with an aerodynamic casing.

Surface-launched depth charges are typically used in a barrage manner in order to cause significant damage through continually battering the submarine with concussive blasts. Depth charges improved considerably since their first employment in World War I. To match improvements in submarine design, pressure-sensing mechanisms and explosives were improved during World War II to provide greater shock power and a charge that would reliably explode over a wide range of depth settings.

Aerial-launched depth bombs are dropped in twos and threes in pre-computed patterns, either from airplanes, helicopters, or blimps. Since aerial attacks normally resulted from surprising the submarine on the surface, air-dropped depth bombs were usually timed to explode at a shallow depth, while the sub was in the process of making a crash dive. In many cases destruction was not achieved, but the submarine was nonetheless forced to retire for repairs.

Early depth charges were designed to be rolled into the water off of the stern of a fast ship. The ship had to be moving fast enough to avoid the concussion of the depth charge blast. Later designs allowed the depth charge to be hurled some distance from the ship, allowing slower ships to operate them and for larger areas to be covered. Today, depth charges not only can be dropped by aircraft or surface ships, but can also be carried by missiles to their target.

Anti-submarine Mortar

With the discovery that depth charges rarely scored a kill by hitting a submarine, but instead were most effective in barrages, it was found that similar or better effects could be obtained by larger numbers of smaller explosions. The anti-submarine mortar is actually an array of spigot mortars, designed to fire off a number of small explosives simultaneously and create an array of explosions around a submarine's position. These were often called *Hedgehogs* after the name given a World War II British design. Later ASW mortar shells were fitted with impact detonators that fired only after actual contact with the hull of the submarine, allowing sonar crews to maintain a constant sound track until a hit was achieved.

The Hedgehog fired twenty four 14.5 kg charges whereas a later development called the "Squid" fired three full-sized depth charges. A further development called "Limbo" was used into the 1960s, and this used 1 ton charges. A development of the Anti-submarine mortar, designed primarily for the exceptionally challenging task of littoral anti-submarine operations, utlizes a shaped charge warhead. An example of this is the Saab Dynamics ASW-600 and the upgraded ASW-601.

The early anti-submarine torpedoes were straight running types and usually a group was fired in case the target manoeuvred. They can be divided into two main types, the heavyweight, fired from submarines, and the lightweight which are fired from ships, dropped from aircraft (both fixed wing and helicopters) and delivered by rocket. Later ones used active/passive sonar homing and wire-guidance. Pattern running and wake-homing torpedoes have also been developed.

The first successful homing torpedo was introduced by the German Navy for use by its U-boat arm against Allied shipping. After capturing several of these weapons, along with independent research, the United States introduced the FIDO air-dropped homing torpedo (also called the Mark 24 'mine' as a cover) in 1943. FIDO was designed to breach the steel pressure hull of a submarine but not necessarily cause a catastrophic implosion, forcing the now-crippled submarine to surface where the submarine and crew might possibly be captured. After World War II, homing torpedoes became one of the primary anti-submarine weapons, used by most of the world's naval powers. Aircraft continued to be a primary launching platform, including the newly available helicopter, though homing torpedoes can also be launched from surface ships or submarines. However, the torpedo's inherent limitations in speed of attack and detection by the target have led to the development of missile-borne anti-submarine weapons that can be delivered practically on top of the enemy submarine, such as ASROC.

On ships the torpedoes are generally launched from a triple-barreled launcher by compressed air. These may be mounted on deck or below. On submarines torpedoes have been carried externally as well as internally. The latter have been launched in the past by stern tubes as well as by the more normal forward ones. Aircraft delivery platforms have included both unmanned helicopters, such as the US DASH, and manned ones such as British Westland Wasp. The helicopter may be solely a weapons carrier or it can have submarine detection facilities.

Mine

Similar to those designed to defeat surface ships, mines can be laid to wait for an enemy submarine to pass by and then explode to cause concussive damage to the submarine. Some are mobile and upon detection they can move towards the submarine until within lethal range. There has even been development of mines that have the ability to launch an encapsulated torpedo at a detected submarine. Mines can be laid by submarines, ships, or aircraft.

Anti-submarine Rocket

One of the latest anti-submarine weapons, Anti-Submarine ROCkets (ASROCs), SUBROC, the Ikara, the French Malafon, and the Italian MILAS differ from other types of missiles in that instead of having a warhead which the missiles delivers to the target directly and explodes, they carry another anti-submarine weapon to a point of the surface where that weapon is dropped in the water to complete the attack. The missile itself launches from its platform and travels to the designated delivery point.

The major advantages of a missile are range and speed of attack. Torpedoes are not very fast compared to a missile, nor as long-ranged, and are much easier for a submarine to detect. Anti-sub missiles are usually delivered from surface vessels, offering the surface escort an all-weather, all-sea-conditions instant readiness weapon to attack time-urgent targets that no other delivery system can match for speed of response. They have the added advantage that they are under the direct control of the escort vessel's commander, and unlike air-delivered weapons cannot be diverted to other taskings, or be dependent on weather or maintenance availability. Aircraft-delivery can be further compromised by low-fuel-state, or an expended weapon load. The missile is always available, and at instant readiness. It allows the torpedo or Nuclear Depth Bomb to enter the water practically on top of the submarine's position, minimizing the submarine's ability to detect and evade the attack. Missiles are also more rapid and accurate in many cases than helicopters or aircraft for dropping torpedoes and depth charges, with a typical interval of 1 to 1.5 minutes from a launch decision to torpedo splashdown. Helicopters frequently take much longer to just get off the escort's deck.

Weapon Control Systems

The readiness of weapons was at first determined manually. Early fire control consisted of range measurements and calculation of the submarines course and speed. The aiming point was then manually determined by rule. Later, mechanical computers were used to solve the fire control problem with electrical indication of weapon readiness. Today the weapon firing process is carried out by digital computer with elaborate displays of all relevant parameters.

ASW Countermeasures

The main countermeasure the submarine has is stealth, that is it tries not to be detected. Against the ASW weapon itself, both active and passive countermeasures are used. The former may be a noise making jammer or a decoy providing a signal that looks like a submarine. Passive countermeasures may consist of coatings to minimise a torpedo's sonar reflections or an outer hull to provide a stand-off from its explosion. The Anti-submarine weapon has to overcome these countermeasures.

MARITIME PATROL AIRCRAFT

A maritime patrol aircraft, also simply patrol aircraft, or by the older term patrol bomber, is a fixed-wing aircraft designed to operate for long durations over water in maritime patrol, anti-shipping, anti-submarine and search and rescue roles. The first aircraft that would now be identified as patrol bombers were flown by the Royal Naval Air Service during World War I, primarily on anti-submarine patrols. At first blimps were the only aircraft capable of staying aloft for the long periods of time (as much as 10 hours) need by the patrols whilst carrying a useful payload. Shorter-range patrols were mounted by adapted bombers such as the Sopwith 1 1/2 Strutter. Later in the war aeroplanes were developed specifically for the role. These were usually large floatplanes such as the Short 184 or flying boats such as the Felixstowe F.2.

Many of the World War II patrol aircraft were converted from long-range bombers or airliners, with notable conversions being Germany's Focke-Wulf Fw 200 and the widespread use of B-24 Liberators during World War II to patrol the areas between Iceland and Greenland and attack German submarines. Purpose-built aircraft were also used, including Britain's Short Sunderland and the American PBY Catalina.

After the war the patrol role was generally taken over by conversions of civilian airliners that had range and performance better than most WWII bon.bers. The latest jet-powered bombers of the 1950s did not have the endurance needed for long, over-water cruising, and more importantly did not have the low loitering speed necessary for anti-submarine operations. The main threat to the United States throughout the 1960s and into the 1980s were Soviet submarines, which were found primarily with the use of sonobuoys, and which then would be attacked with homing torpedoes. Today the threat of a large scale submarine attack is remote, and many forces are downsizing their patrol aircraft fleets. Those still in service are used primarily for counter-smuggling and Exclusive Economic Zone enforcement duties.

Sensors

Maritime patrol aircraft are typically fitted with a wide range of sensors:

- *Radar* to detect surface shipping movements;
- *Magnetic Anomaly Detector* (MAD) to detect submarine movements. The MAD detecting head is typically mounted on an extension from the tail to minimize magnetic interference with the MAD;
- *Sonobuoy* dropped from the aircraft into the sea to detect submarines, transmitting the data back to the aircraft for analysis;
- *ELINT sensors* to monitor civilian and military telecommunications;
- *Infrared camera* are also useful in monitoring shipping movements.

A maritime patrol aircraft typically carries a dozen or so crew members, including relief flight crews, to effectively operate the equipment for up to 12 hours at a time.

Examples of Maritime Patrol Aircraft / ASW Aircraft

- Supermarine Southampton
- Blackburn Perth

World War II Era

- Consolidated PBY Catalina (USA)
- Consolidated PB2Y Coronado (USA)
- Consolidated PB4Y-2 Privateer (USA)
- Dornier Do 24 (Netherlands, Germany)
- Focke-Wulf Fw 200 *Condor* (Germany)
- Junkers Ju 290 (Germany)
- Kawanishi H6K *Mavis* (Japan)
- Kawanishi H8K *Emily* (Japan)

- Lockheed Ventura (USA)
- Martin PBM Mariner (USA)
- Short Sunderland (UK)
- SB2U Vindicator (USA)

Cold War and Modern Eras

- Avro Shackleton (UK)
- Beriev Be-10 (USSR)
- Beriev Be-12 (USSR)
- Boeing P-8 Poseidon (USA)
- Breguet Alizé (France) (Carrier based ASW)
- Breguet Atlantique (France)
- CASA CN-235 Persuader (Spain)
- CASA C-295 Persuader (Spain)
- Canadair CP-107 Argus (Canada)
- Fairey Gannet (UK) (Carrier based ASW)
- Fokker F-27 Maritime (Netherlands)
- Grumman AF Guardian (USA) (Carrier based ASW)
- Grumman S-2 Tracker (USA) (Carrier based ASW)
- Hawker-Siddeley Nimrod (UK)
- Ilyushin Il-38 (USSR)
- Lockheed P-2 Neptune (USA)
- Lockheed P-3 Orion (USA)
  - CP-140 Aurora (Canada)
  - CP-140A Arcturus (Canada)
- Lockheed S-3 Viking (US) (Carrier based ASW)
- Martin P5M Marlin (USA)
- PZL M28B Bryza 1R, 1RMbis, 1E (Poland)
- Tupolev Tu-142 (USSR)
- HESA IrAn-140 (Iran)

MAGNETIC ANOMALY DETECTOR

A magnetic anomaly detector (MAD) is an instrument used to detect minute variations in the Earth's magnetic field. The term refers specifically to magnetometers used by military forces to detect submarines (a mass of ferromagnetic material creates a detectable disturbance in the magnetic field); the military MAD gear is a descendent of geomagnetic survey instruments used to search for minerals by the disturbance of the normal earth-field.

Geoexploration by measuring and studying variations in the Earth's magnetic field has been conducted by scientists since 1843. The first uses of magnetometers were for the location of ore deposits. Thalen's 'The Examination of Iron Ore Deposits by Magnetic Measurements', published in 1879, was the first scientific treatise describing this practical use.

Magnetic anomaly detectors employed to detect submarines during World War II harnessed the fluxgate magnetometer, an inexpensive and easy to use technology developed in the 1930s by Victor Vacquier of Gulf Oil for finding ore deposits. MAD gear was used by both Japanese and U.S. anti-submarine forces, either towed by ship or mounted in aircraft to detect shallow submerged enemy submarines. The Japanese called the technology *jikitanchiki*(Áxl¢cåw_j, "Magnetic Detector"). After the war, the U.S. Navy continued to develop MAD gear as a parallel development with sonar detection technologies.

Operation

To reduce interference from electrical equipment or metal in the fuselage of the aircraft, the MAD sensor is placed at the end of a boom or a towed aerodynamic device. Even so, the submarine must be very near the aircraft's position and close to the sea surface for detection of the change or anomaly. The size of the submarine and its hull composition determine the detection range. MAD devices are usually mounted on aircraft.

Function

There is some misunderstanding of the mechanism of detection of submarines in water using the MAD boom system. Magnetic moment displacement is ostensibly the main disturbance, yet submarines are detectable even when oriented parallel to the Earth's magnetic field, despite construction with non-ferromagnetic hulls. For example, the Soviet-Russian Alfa class submarine, whose hull is constructed out of titanium to give dramatic submerged performance and protection from detection by MAD sensors, is still detectable.

The Alfa's detectability has led some analysts to deduce that the MAD's name is an intentional deception, so effective that the Soviet Union decided to construct the Alfa and even consider building the Typhoon class submarine SSBN out of titanium at one point. Since titanium structures are detectable, MAD sensors do not directly detect deviations in the Earth's magnetic field. Instead, they may be described as long-range electric and electromagnetic field detector arrays of great sensitivity.

An electric field is set up in conductors experiencing a variation in physical environmental conditions, providing that they are contiguous and possess sufficient mass. Particularly in submarine hulls, there is a measurable temperature difference between the bottom and top of the hull producing a related salinity difference, as salinity is affected by temperature of water. The difference in salinity creates an electric potential across the hull. An electric current then flows through the hull, between the laminae of seawater separated by depth and temperature. The resulting dynamic electric field produces an electromagnetic field of its own, and thus even a titanium hull will be detectable on a MAD scope, as will a surface ship for the same reason.

Other Uses

For geomagnetic survey work the detector can be mounted on a long probe in front of the aircraft or be a towed device. A chart is produced that geologists can study to determine the location and extent of mineral deposits.

During the Vietnam War the original AC-130A Spectre gunships employed the "Pave Mace"/"Black Crow" magnetic anomaly detection system to detect truck ignition coils in vehicles hidden under heavy jungle canopies. When the electric current flowing through such a coil changes it produces a magnetic flux, which is, in simplest terms, a change in the magnetic field over a given area. In particular, when the trucks were turned on the current flowing through the coils went from zero to some maximum, producing a large and easily detectable flux.